Van Gogh

PORTRAIT OF THE ARTIST DEDICATED TO GAUGUIN. SEPTEMBER 1888.
FOGG MUSEUM OF ART, HARVARD UNIVERSITY, CAMBRIDGE, MASS.

Van Gogh

A STUDY OF HIS LIFE AND WORK BY
FRANK ELGAR

Frederick A. Praeger Publishers

NEW YORK

TRANSLATED FROM THE FRENCH BY

JAMES CLEUGH

THE PUBLISHERS WOULD LIKE TO EXPRESS THEIR THANKS
TO ENGINEER V. W. VAN GOGH
FOR HIS ASSISTANCE IN THE PREPARATION OF THIS WORK
MR A. M. HAMMACHER
DIRECTOR OF THE KRÖLLER-MÜLLER RIJKSMUSEUM
OTTERLO
MR W. J. B. SANDBERG
DIRECTOR OF THE STEDELIJK MUSEUM AMSTERDAM
THE PUBLISHERS OF 'CERCLE D'ART'
FOR THE LOAN OF COLOUR PHOTOGRAPHS
AND TO THOSE COLLECTORS WHO GAVE THEIR PERMISSION
TO PHOTOGRAPH WORKS IN THEIR POSSESSION.

THE PRODUCTION OF THIS BOOK WAS SUPERVISED BY
ROBERT MAILLARD
COLOUR PHOTOGRAPHY BY
WALTER DRÄYER ZURICH AND ANNA WACHSMANN NEW YORK
TEXT SET IN GREAT BRITAIN BY
THE CAMELOT PRESS SOUTHAMPTON
ENGRAVINGS MADE BY BUSSIÈRE ET NOUEL
PRINTED IN FRANCE
DESIGN BY RENÉ BEN SUSSAN

THE ROAD. 1881. V. W. VAN GOGH COLLECTION, LAREN

VINCENT was born on the 30th March 1853, at Zundert, a village of three thousand inhabitants near the Belgian frontier in Brabant, Holland. His father, Theodore, the pastor of the village, was himself the son of a pastor who had had twelve children. Three of Vincent's uncles were picture-dealers, one of them, also called Vincent, carrying on his business at The Hague.

Theodore and his wife, Anna Carbentus, had six children, three sons, Vincent and Theo, who was four years the younger, Cornélis and three daughters, Anna, Elisabeth and Wilhelmina. The family was a most united one, like many others in a country where the domestic virtues and adherence to Christian doctrine are the foundations of society. Like so many others, too, in Holland, the van

9

Goghs were middle-class citizens living narrow and monotonous lives, still further restricted by Calvinist austerity. Such families often dread the emergence in their midst of some rebellious member likely at any moment to shatter the rigid framework of the home and destroy its unity, an adventurer destined to carve an empire from the ends of the earth, a scientist who may later revolutionise the laws of physics, a thinker who breaks new ground or an artist whose turbulent genius will scandalise his native land before it comes to idolise him.

Vincent was extremely sensitive. Even the impressions made on him as a child were never forgotten. No doubt his earliest years profoundly influenced his character, while his passion for devotion and self-sacrifice originated in his religious reading and the exemplary domesticity of his parents implanted in him the ambition, never relinquished and never realised, to found a family himself. Even in his moments of deepest depression he never ceased to ask for news of his mother and his brothers and sisters. Throughout all the adverse chances and changes of his wandering life he retained a warm and constant recollection of the people and things he had known as a boy. To his mother in her old age he wrote from St. Remy: 'I've never stopped looking like a Zundert villager, Toon or Piet Prins, for instance. It sometimes seems to me as though I feel and think just as they do.' To his brother Theo he wrote: 'We shall always have something of the fields and moors of Brabant in us.' Wherever he went he never forgot the humble parsonage, the dismal village and commonplace society into which he had been born. His imagination endowed them with poetic enchantment. His voluminous correspondence proves his vigilant affection for his relatives and his unvarying attachment to his friends. Such was the man so often described as unstable, fickle and inconstant.

His father and his sister Elisabeth said that he lived among his family and fellow-citizens 'as if he were a foreigner'. But in fact it was not so. Neither his father, his sister nor anyone of their kind in so remote a community, with its dull, everyday existence, its paltry preoccupations and its social and religious conformity, was capable of understanding him. All his biographers agree that in

CANAL BANK. 1880-1881. V. W. VAN GOGH COLLECTION, LAREN

boyhood and youth he was sturdy, tough and plucky, observant of what went on about him and quick to realise its essential nature, while indulgent to the weak and simple-minded. Later on he was attracted by women and sought the friendship of men. He loved country life. In his long walks across the fields and marshes of Brabant he watched birds, gathered plants and brought home insects to collect and study. He therefore seems to have been perfecturely normal, both physically and mentally.

And yet quite a different light has been thrown upon his character. We are told that he was a short, thick-set boy with red hair and strangely green eyes, awkward and clumsy, with uncivilised and solitary habits, so much so that his brother and sisters were afraid to accompany him on his walks. His timid and slow-witted father, alarmed by his son's independent cast of mind, incessant curiosity and keen sensibility, regarded the boy with morose disapproval. The family felt Vincent to be an intruder and avoided intimacy with him. They thus encouraged the isolated, uncouth and vagabond existence they believed he preferred by nature. Such is the origin of the legend which has survived all critical investigation of the real facts. The child was actually sociable, affectionate and expansive with a special sympathy for unfortunate persons. Yet he was perpetually being rebuffed. His patience and gentleness were profound. Yet he has been called irritable and temperamental. He wanted to live at peace with other people and to work with other artists. Yet it is alleged that he disliked everybody. He is supposed to have been capricious, incalculable and self-centred. Yet he was always a loyal friend and could be wonderfully sympathetic with those who did not discourage his dealings with them. His letters to Theo, to van Rappard, to Gauguin and to Emile Bernard prove it. No one, in any case, has ever been steadier in his aims, sentiments and passions and less obstinate in bearing a grudge. He was always ready to forget the most cruel wrongs he suffered.

His abrupt manners, uncompromising candour and sudden changes of mood may well have been disconcerting. But if his early youth had not been deprived of trust and tenderness, if he had grown up in a different environment, among more emancipated

THE ROOFS. VIEW FROM VAN GOGH'S STUDIO IN THE SCHENKWEG.
JULY 1882. G. RENAND COLLECTION, PARIS.

and charitable people, instead of finding his natural impulsiveness confronted by so restricted a social horizon with its crushing discipline and petty tyrannies, he would almost certainly have developed a more genial character.

It is doubtful whether anyone appreciated his virtues and needs as a child. Most poets and artists revenge themselves upon society for their early humiliations. But Vincent always blamed himself alone for his sufferings. A frustrated and misunderstood child, not given its due meed of affection, ends as a man without roots, in rebellion or bewilderment, almost always embittered. Such were Poussin, Cézanne and van Gogh, sufferers who made others suffer. 'One may have a blazing hearth in one's soul', wrote Vincent, 'and yet no one ever comes to sit by it. Passers by only see a wisp of smoke rising from the chimney and continue on their way.'

13

MARSHLAND. JUNE 1881. J. P. SCHOLTE-VAN HOUTEN, LOCHEM

The innocence, isolation and irreconcilability of such men render them shy of society. Van Rappard said of Vincent that 'he was utterly at a loss in everyday life, perpetually making blunders. His conception of life, as of art, was majestic and unselfish, adding to the awe and admiration he inspired . . . yet I felt more respect than friendship, more veneration than fellow-feeling, for his wild and extravagant character.' The fact is that friendship and fellow-feeling are in general withheld from individualist of this type, though their human qualities deserve such appreciation. Esteem, not sympathy, is their lot. They are reverenced, but not loved. They are little envied. But they are feared. We find it hard to value at their true worth those who are superior to ourselves, invade our comfort and announce truths which discredit those we ourselves support. Many of the errors, lies and unjust actions in the world arise in this way.

Most biographies of Vincent present him as an eccentric creature, afflicted by melancholia and mania, a 'crackpot' inevitably doomed to lunacy. It is perfectly true that under the lash of his repeated disappointments and physical and moral sufferings Vincent ended by losing the balance of his mind and sanity. But most healthy persons would have succumbed at an even earlier date to so much tribulation. It is more reasonable to wonder at his extraordinary capacity for resistance, exceeding even those of Hölderlin and Nietzsche, his brothers in affliction. From his birth until the pistol-shot at Auvers he retained bodily and mental vigour. For the greater part of his life he was compassionate and generous, devoid

YOUNG PEASANT WITH SCYTHE. OCTOBER 1881.
KRÖLLER-MÜLLER RIJKSMUSEUM, OTTERLO

'I have resumed work with the living model. For this purpose I have been able to secure various people, notably Piet Kaufmann, the labourer. . . . I have learnt to measure distance, see and look for main lines.'   Letter to Theo

of hypocrisy as of pride, as discreet as he was scrupulous, incapable of either envy or hate, of seeing ugliness or mediocrity anywhere. He could despair but never resent. Though industrious and resolute, he was never unsociable except by compulsion. Such were the essential components of his nature, which subsisted almost to the end.

But his contemporaries may be excused for seeing him in a different light. 'In a world of made-up faces the untouched complexion looks rouged.' André Gide's apt observation is relevant here. For the most striking feature of the life, writings and painting of Vincent is their complete and utter sincerity, which morality itself tends to condemn in so uncompromising a form. It may be surmised that such sincerity as Vincent's caused him a great deal of annoyance and disappointment. He was only too sincere. The phrase is echoed by the 'human, all too human' of the most outspoken of philosophers, who resembled Vincent in this respect. But the latter's sincerity came perfectly natural to him. It is for this reason that so disturbing an accent of truth is revealed in every one of his gestures, exclamations and works, finding an involuntary and profoundly sympathetic response in all of us. The idea that so noble-minded, courageous and innocent a man should have suffered so much at the hands of others that he was obliged to steel himself to the supreme sacrifice can now only affect us with shame or remorse.

In considering the extent to which his childhood was responsible for the development of his personality, we must remember the domestic discipline to which he was subjected, his religious reading and the rustics by whom he was surrounded, with their primitive habits, poverty and harsh outlook. Such factors increased Vincent's individualism. Obedience to social conventions in these circumstances would have amounted to a betrayal of the reality he sought to define. He repudiated in his maturity the early experiences which had so deeply impressed him. Yet he always spoke of them with great reserve. They included little in the way of formal education. But he read the English and French classics with deep admiration. So highly organised an intelligence as his needed no tuition. Submission to it would have meant taking advice or

GIRL IN FOREST. SEPTEMBER 1882. KRÖLLER-MÜLLER RIJKSMUSEUM, OTTERLO.

enduring tyranny, with consequent prejudice to his genius. By being self-taught he was enabled to comply with the promptings of his own impulses, to preserve the primal vigour of his instincts and the plenitude of his resources. He does not seem to have owed to any individual the release of the extremely rare gifts he possessed and the opportunities to apply them. For Vincent might just as easily have become a thinker, a poet, a hero or a saint as a painter. It may be thought, in fact, that he became all these at once.

In any case, few philosophers, writers or artists have ever felt and expressed so acutely the dramatic elements of the human predicament or set themselves with more determination to come to terms with it in their lives and works. It will therefore be of interest to study the life and the works of Vincent in order to discover whether he succeeded or failed in his search for absolute truth, a conception which has always obsessed mankind and never more so than to-day.

AT sixteen he was given a post as salesman in the art gallery formerly managed by his Uncle Vincent at The Hague but by then transferred by the latter to the Parisian firm of Goupil. The boy stayed in this gallery for four years, leaving it in May 1873 for the London branch. There he soon fell in love with his landlady's daughter, Ursula. He proposed to her, was rejected and became so depressed that he returned to his family in Holland. He remained at home for four months before being sent, in October 1874, to the Goupil Gallery in Paris. But he did not forget Ursula amid the distractions of the French capital. On being returned by his employers to their London branch, he made an attempt to renew acquaintance with the girl, met with a second refusal and was recalled by the firm to Paris, where he arrived, in a state of desperation, on the 15th May, 1875. Thenceforward he performed his duties at the gallery at first with indifference, later with sullen irritation. Even while in London he had declined to advise customers to purchase any prints he objected to. In Paris, too, his fundamental honesty rebelled against what he considered organised fraud by the dealers in works of art. Meanwhile, his disappointment in love had turned his thoughts to a kind of fanatical religious mysticism. He read the Bible constantly. He attended churches and other places of worship, including synagogues. As he proved incapable of complying with the requirements of trade, he was eventually dismissed, in April 1876, from his employment. He then tried to earn a living, first as an assistant schoolmaster at Ramsgate in England, and, secondly, as a lay preacher under the Methodist pastor at Isleworth. It was at that time, apparently, that he first discovered the wretched condition of the urban labouring class. On the 31st December he visited his parents at Etten, to which place his father had been appointed on the 22nd October 1875. Three weeks later he went to work in a bookshop at Dordrecht, but again failed to make a success of the job. His mind turned more and more to the prospects of a religious vocation. On the 8th May 1877 he left for Amsterdam to study for the entrance examination at a theological college, hoping that he had at last found the way to a congenial calling. But after fourteen months of work which proved as unprofitable as it had been intensely

MAN SWEEPING. 1881.
KRÖLLER-MÜLLER RIJKSMUSEUM,
OTTERLO

MAN DIGGING.
1882.
V. W. VAN GOGH COLLECTION, LAREN

pursued he was obliged to give it up, and returned in despair to Etten.

His father's exasperation may be imagined. As already stated, the pastor's intelligence was limited. His piety and virtuous behaviour did not mean that he was truly religious and good. He did not know what to do with a son who could not learn a trade and refused to be taught anything else. The young man only seemed willing to educate himself in solitude or 'free of charge at the great university of the poor'. He wanted to be a preacher, serving only Christ. The father, weary of argument, had him enrolled for a three months' course at the Brussels school for evangelists. In December, without waiting for an appointment—of which he was to be apprised a month later—he went off to the Borinage district of Belgium, intent on revealing the light of the gospel to those who most needed it, miners living in extreme poverty and engaged in the hardest possible work. He flattered himself, with the touching presumption of a novice, that he was capable of bringing consolation and the Christian faith to these outcasts.

It was then that he began his apostolic career, the distressing episodes of which are so well known. He spent himself with selfless generosity, teaching the children, tending the sick, distributing his scanty possessions, money, clothing and furniture. He overflowed with love, less for God, if the truth must be told, than for mankind. Yet in spite of all his efforts to prove his compassion and devotion to the miners, he did not succeed in convincing them. Moreover, since he was an indifferent speaker, his preaching had no effect on these unfortunate people, whom he had thought the most likely of all to listen to him. Whatever advances and sacrifices he made, he was no better understood by the Borain proletariat than he had been by his own family. His anxious longing to communicate with and be received by and among them met only with repeated rebuffs, which threw him back, time after time, into his irremediable solitude. It was even questionable whether these hapless creatures would have agreed to an improvement of their lot. Bernardin de St. Pierre used to say that he had never met any human being who did not revel in his own misery. Vincent stripped himself of everything he had and made himself the poorest

STUDY OF TREE. APRIL 1882. KRÖLLER-MÜLLER RIJKSMUSEUM, OTTERLO
'The other, Roots, *represents roots of trees in sandy soil. I have now tried to give the landscape the same feeling as the model, as though clinging to the ground in the same convulsive and passionate manner and yet torn out of it by the gale.*'
Letter to Theo

of the poor. He even blackened his face so as to look just like the rest of them. But whatever he did he remained a stranger among the miners. On the contrary, his extravagant charity merely bewildered them. He saw that he would never be accepted. But he was to congratulate himself later on for having converted a confirmed drunkard and cured by his assiduous nursing, a patient who had been given up by the doctors.

He was obliged to leave the bakery at which he lodged and live in a wooden hut, where he slept beside a wretched fire after the exhausting labours of the day. These self-inflicted privations injured his health. To crown all his misfortunes, his excessive zeal, far from being approved by the Protestant hierarchy, prejudiced it against him. The circumstances were reported to the Consistory Court, which cancelled his appointment. Vincent's instinct for justice was too strong for him to yield tamely to the decision. 'Churchmen', he wrote to Theo, 'have a long established academic tradition which is often detestable . . . they are encased in a steel armour of prejudice and convention.' When they ventured to recommend obedience and resignation, 'I answered, Leave me alone. They considered that most disrespectful. Resignation is for those who can manage it. Faith is for those who can believe.'

After Vincent's dismissal, Theo visited him on behalf of the family. It is easy to guess the turn taken by the interview between the two brothers, the younger still so full of middle-class sagacity, the elder so devoted to truth and magnanimous, resenting the advice of ordinary common sense almost as if it were an insult. Why not choose another profession? Theo may have urged. Go in for some decent, sound business, that of an accountant, for instance, a carpenter or even a baker. Vincent ought to think of the trouble and worry he is causing his family. He must realise

FISH DRYING (LA SÉCHERIE DE LIMANDES). MAY 1882.
KRÖLLER-MÜLLER RIJKSMUSEUM, OTTERLO

ROAD NEAR LOOSDUINEN. JULY 1882. V. W. VAN GOGH COLLECTION, LAREN

that it will not be able to support him if he will 'persist in behaving like someone with a private income'. But it may be doubted whether such remonstrances had any effect on a being so defence-less and disinterested as Vincent. In any case, he decided to stay where he was. He gave the reason in a letter dated the 15th October 1879. 'Please note that if I am playing the independent gentleman I am doing it rather oddly. I don't quite know how to rebut the charge. But I should be sorry if you did not come to modify your point of view one of these days.'

He had been given such advice often enough in the past. When-ever he had followed it, the result had been disastrous. He still remembered his experiences at Amsterdam, the worst he had ever known. The uncertainties of his present existence seemed quite agreeable in comparison. But he could not bear to think of being

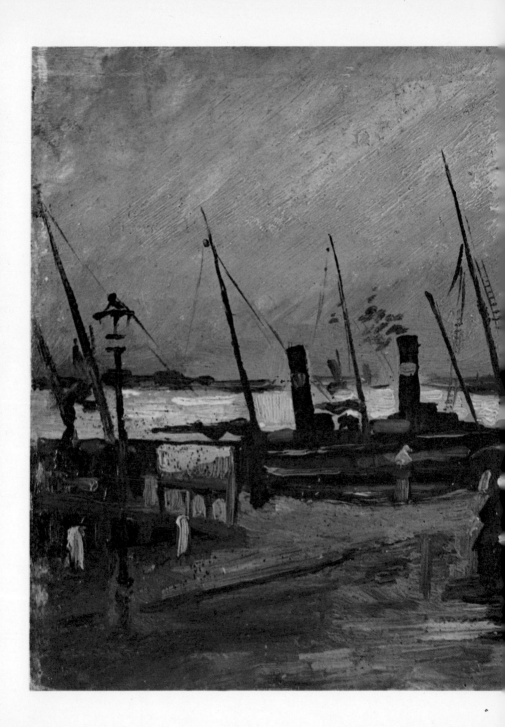

QUAY AT ANTWERP.
DECEMBER 1885. V. W.
VAN GOGH COLLECTION,
LAREN

'*If I'm not worth anything now, I shan't be worth any more later on; but if in future I'm found to be worth something I'm worth as much to-day. For corn is corn even if city folk think it's grass at first.*'
Letter to Theo

OLD MAN WITH AN UMBRELLA. OCTOBER 1882.
MR AND MRS JOHN REWALD COLLECTION, NEW YORK

a drag on his family, of being regarded as a lazybones, a good-for-nothing. If it were really so, 'I shouldn't care to stay much longer in this world'. This distressing letter must be read to the end if we mean to penetrate the most secret recesses of Vincent's mind, where his fate was already written. Though greatly discouraged by what was being thought of him, he still had some hopes for the future. 'It may be', he adds, 'that we shall see one another more clearly and understand one another better one day.' He compares his state of mind with the changing seasons of the year. 'Sooner or later the hard frost ends, whether we are glad of it or not, and one fine morning the wind blows from another direction and a thaw comes.' If he had not felt an interior conviction of genius, he would scarcely have had the strength to resist so much humiliation and suffering. He would not have 'stayed longer in this world'. He would have fired there and then the shot which was to set him free eleven years later. But far more then eleven years have been needed to prove him right and his family, the world and the rationalists wrong.

He did not write to Theo again for nine months, a period darkened by the most utter material and moral wretchedness. His wanderings at that time tell us nothing of his changed thoughts and feelings. But when he again communicated with Theo in July 1880 he wrote that he was now a different man. He compared his recent past with the moulting season in birds. 'They may continue in that condition or emerge from it as if reborn.'

What was the nature of this rebirth? He had broken his ties with religion, his country and his family, though he had by no means disowned them, for he retained 'a sort of loyalty in disloyalty'. He still believed, of course, in God. But he had done with evangelists incapable of human feeling, insensible as drunkards in the face of spiritual reality. As for his family, he no more trusted it now than it trusted him, though he still hoped for a genuine reconciliation one day. His country in future was to be only that of painting, books and works of art. 'In my exile I am often homesick, but for the land of pictures alone.' It would be still more accurate to say that art had replaced country, family and religion in him. 'Try to understand', he wrote, 'the most profound utterances of the great, dedicated artists in their masterpieces, for you will find God there.'

Although this period may superficially appear barren, there is no doubt that it worked a great change in him. In a phrase of Nietzsche's, almost identical with that then employed by Vincent, 'the wind of thaw' had been felt by this unhappy man, whom misfortune itself had rehabilitated. Vincent gives a clear explanation of his interior revolution. He may seem to be lazy, faint-hearted and a social failure. 'But I feel instinctively', he declares, 'that I am good for something, that there is some point in my existence, that I could become quite a different person. What use could I be, then? What service could I perform? There is something in me. But what is it?' He begged his brother: 'I should be so happy if you could somehow come to see something better than an idler in me.'

He had every right to reject so insulting a description. For he had barely recovered from the agonies of a self-induced birth before becoming a new man, ready to defy adversity and a despair that had threatened his life. For if there had been no such vigorous revival of his spirit he would never have been able to survive the ruin of his mystical ambitions. He himself, once more, informs us how he managed to recoil from the brink of catastrophe. He did so by trying to turn his own passions to account. The man who was to execute, during the decade of life that still remained to him, a vast body of work which our century continues to wonder at, cannot be called an idler, nor one who even then gave up all his spare time to apostolic work and also found opportunities to educate himself by reading, form his own taste and teach himself to draw. He had started making rough sketches as early as 1878 in Brussels. He resumed this activity in the Borinage district. But it was only after being obliged to abandon his evangelical labours that he seriously took up drawing, first as a copyist and later with the intense application that his iron will dictated. His models were miners and weavers. In the summer of 1880, working in the nursery of a Cuesmes miner, he copied engravings by Jules Breton and Millet. He procured manuals of anatomy and perspective.

On the 15th October in that year he settled in Brussels, living on the pittance of sixty francs a month reluctantly sent him by his

THE WIDOW. APRIL 1882.　　　　　　　THE OLD SAILOR. FEBRUARY 1883

KRÖLLER-MÜLLER RIJKSMUSEUM, OTTERLO

father. Luckily, Theo came to his assistance, providing him with money, books and works of art, which Vincent copied industriously. He cut his living expenses to take lessons in perspective. It was then, at the beginning of November, that he met van Rappard, and soon began to share his studio. Van Rappard described him as 'A sombre fanatic who toiled and struggled, could very often lose his temper and become violent, and yet was always worthy of friendship and admiration owing to the nobility of his character and his great gifts as an artist.'

On van Rappard's departure for Utrecht Vincent took refuge, on the 12th April 1881, with his parents at Etten. They had at last been persuaded by Theo to allow him to take his chance. Mauve, a well-known painter of the day, whose advice Vincent had asked at The Hague also gave him definite encouragement. Vincent resumed work with renewed ardour, devouring the English and French books in his father's library, drawing labourers (Cat. 1), peasants (Cat. 3 and 6) and a few landscapes, notably the *Mills Near Dordrecht* (Cat. 4). His family and friends were just beginning to be pleased with his evident determination to pursue some aim in life when the tranquillity of the parsonage was shattered by an act of sentimental folly on his part.

That summer a cousin named Kee came to spend a holiday at Etten. She was the widowed daughter, with a son four years old, of his Uncle Stricker, a pastor. Vincent fell deeply in love with her and proposed. It was a perfectly natural proceeding. He was twenty-eight and desired to found a family, so as to put an end to the loneliness that tormented him. But just as Ursula, in London in 1874, had refused him, so now did his cousin. She stated that she had promised to remain faithful to the memory of her husband.

VAN GOGH'S FAMILY HOME AT NUENEN (HIS STUDIO ON THE RIGHT). EARLY 1884. PRIVATE COLLECTION, CANADA

THE GARDEN OF THE PRESBYTERY AT NUENEN. WINTER. MARCH 1884
V. W. VAN GOGH COLLECTION, LAREN

Moreover, her parents were utterly opposed to the idea of a
penniless son-in-law, with no settled work and, of all things, an
artist. Vincent might have foreseen his rejection. When he first
mentioned the subject to the young woman, she had exclaimed
in horror: 'No, never! I couldn't think of it!' Yet he was so
persistent that in the end she fled to her father in Amsterdam.

He wrote to her again and again. She did not answer his letters.
At last he could stand it no longer and set off, in December, to see
her. But when he called at the house she declined to appear. He
insisted for two days, with an obstinacy described by his uncle
as 'disgusting', on seeing her. Eventually he held his open hand
over a lighted lamp on the table and said he would keep it there
till she arrived. Her horrified parents saw the flame begin to burn

the motionless flesh. But the enraged pastor declared: "Never! Never!" At last Vincent fainted.

This act of voluntary sacrifice can hardly be regarded as anything but symbolic. In the same way, when he cut off his ear seven years later and on the 27th July 1890, committed suicide, both these actions seem to have been intensified repetitions of the behaviour in 1881. Normally, a lover blinded by passion takes vengeance on the woman who rejects him. Vincent, on the other hand, like Orestes, turns his revenge upon himself, regarded as the guilty party, unworthily claiming a partner beyond his reach. And if we penetrate further into the secrets of this fastidious mind, we may well believe that he first burned, then mutilated and finally killed himself so as to suffer in his own person the pain and injustice inflicted by the world. We must remember that in spite of his resentment of the God of the pastors he always remained conscious of the Jesus he had imagined as a child. It was to that compassionate and loving God that he had dedicated his thoughts and deeds. It was with Christ that he identified himself when he exclaimed, after the tragic affair in Amsterdam, 'My God, my God, why hast Thou forsaken me?'

He returned to Etten in an indescribable state of despair. The only consolation he found there took the form of remonstrances and warnings against sin. 'Is it a sin to love?' he exclaimed. 'To have need of love, not to be able to live without it?' Why could he not enjoy his share of happiness and discover 'real life'? If his cousin had returned his passion, he would undoubtedly have been cured of his instability and melancholy. Should we then have lost a great artist? Nothing is less certain. As his sister-in-law, Mme. van Gogh-Bönger, said later, the foundation of a family would have encouraged him to win his independence, but as it was 'he bade farewell to all ambition and thenceforward lived only for his work'.

The Amsterdam disappointment, accordingly, decisively influenced his remaining years and the work he still had to do. From that time on he made no further attempt to choose a wife, acquire a position in society or live on his own resources. Nor did he try seriously to avoid falling into poverty. He continued to depend on others. He never achieved freedom as a man, even after he had

AVENUE OF POPLARS. MARCH 1884. V. W. VAN GOGH COLLECTION, LAREN.

WOMAN DIGGING. 1885. V. W. VAN GOGH COLLECTION, LAREN

achieved it as an artist. Meanwhile, arguments with his father at
Etten grew more frequent. The pastor taxed him with 'impiety', by
which he meant that Vincent was not devout. Since breaking with
the Church he had not attended services. On Christmas Day the
most violent of all their quarrels broke out and Vincent had to leave
the parsonage. He went to The Hague, where he hoped to take
advantage of the advice of Mauve. He had scarcely arrived before
he met, in the street, a woman calling herself Christine. She was an
ugly, faded creature, and pregnant, a prostitute. Vincent made her
his mistress and used her as a model. It is to be noted that he had
not forgotten his Cousin Kee. He still loved and always would
love her, in spite of the ignoble Christine. It did not matter to him
which of them he had. It was woman in the abstract that he desired.
It was womanly love, a human presence, that the self-styled recluse

WOMAN PLANTING. 1885. NATIONAL GALLERY, OSLO

BOOTS WITH LACES. 1886. V. W. VAN GOGH COLLECTION, LAREN.

needed. And the more unhappy, poor and fallen a human being
may be, he considered, the more solicitude and compassion should
be shown to such a person. 'It is impossible to forsake a woman',
he said, 'when she is a mother and has been deserted.'

When he described this adventure to Theo he knew that his
brother was going to be shocked. Nevertheless, he made no
attempt to excuse his conduct. 'If there is anything I bitterly regret,
it is that I allowed myself to be distracted for a while by abstract
considerations of mysticism and theology.' His tone is no longer
that of an evangelist, but of a humanitarian. 'The stimulus, the
spark that we need, is love, but certainly not mystical love.' He
made it quite clear what he thought of Christine. 'It was not the
first time I had indulged in the caprice of affection, yes, of affection
and love, for this class of women, cursed, damned and covered with
abuse by the pastors from their pulpits. Personally, I neither curse

BOOTS. 1887. CONE COLLECTION, MUSEUM OF ART, BALTIMORE.

nor damn nor despise them. I am thirty, you know. Do you really suppose I have never wanted to be loved myself?'

In the same letter he wrote: 'The world seems more cheerful if, when we wake up in the morning, we find we are no longer alone and that there is another human being beside us in the half-dark. That's more cheerful than shelves of edifying books and the white-washed walls of a church. . . .'

The sight of so degraded and tarnished a creature must undoubtedly have been distressing enough. But Vincent saw her with his mind's eye. He felt, moreover, that it was urgently necessary to fill the void of his existence, revive his energy and set briskly to work. In reality his connection with this woman, for all its incongruity, renewed his zest for life and inspired him with the ardent desire to create. 'I see pictures and drawings in the most squalid little corners. I am irresistibly impelled to study them.' He

THE FARM. 1885. V. W. VAN GOGH COLLECTION, LAREN

cared little what might be said of him. 'I am pretty indifferent to all that chatter about good and evil, morality and immorality. The fact of the matter is, I can't always see in every case what is good or evil, moral or immoral.'

He applied again to Mauve, who found him a studio in the Schenkweg and gave him the benefit of long experience. Vincent was accordingly by now in a position to develop his gifts and learn his trade as a painter. But his mind was too innocent, noble and fastidious to allow him to plod quietly along the road to success and obtain it by easy means. Mauve's condescending and academic attitude irritated him. One day, when the former had given him a plaster cast of Apollo to copy, Vincent, in a fit of exasperation, seized the cast and threw it on the floor, where it broke. After

STUDIES (WITH THE TOWER AT NUENEN). 1885.
KRÖLLER-MÜLLER RIJKSMUSEUM, OTTERLO

THE POTATO-EATERS. APRIL-MAY 1885. V. W. VAN GOGH COLLECTION, LAREN

'I intended to keep conscientiously in mind the suggestion to the spectator that these people eating their potatoes under the lamp and putting their hands in the plate, have also tilled the soil, so that my picture praises both manual labour and the food they have themselves so honestly procured. I intended that the painting should make people think of a way of life entirely different from our own civilised one. So I have no wish whatever for anybody to consider the work beautiful or good.

'In painting these peasants I thought of what had been said of those of Millet, that they "seem to have been painted with the very soil they sow".'

Letter to Theo

41

thus quarrelling with Mauve, he proceeded to quarrel with the other Hague painters whose company he had sought. In his permanent need for warm human relations, he had dreamed of forming associations with them. But his illusions in this respect were soon dispelled by their petty ambitions, their contemptible rivalries and their unworthy concessions to the tastes of prospective purchasers. Vincent had a loftier idea of the function of an artist. He consulted Tersteeg, a family friend in charge of the local branch of the firm of Goupil. Tersteeg bought one of his drawings, advising him, however, to concoct pretty water-colours, always a popular line, instead of turning out such gloomy and pointless stuff, in which he was wasting his talent. Tersteeg added that he should give up the useless and fatiguing process of working with a model.

Vincent was speechless with fury at the idea that he, with his passion for ever-increasing intimacy with nature and his fellowmen, should work without a model and strive to please when so much suffering had to be endured to get at the truth. Fortunately, his Uncle Cornelius, in business as an art dealer in Amsterdam, ordered twelve small pen drawings from him, views of The Hague. He promised to pay 2.50 florins apiece for them and said he would buy more of the same kind if Vincent would produce them. But on receipt of the first consignment he frankly told his nephew he was disappointed. He had expected more pleasing subjects and more delicate treatment (see Cat. 9, *Behind the Schenkweg*). He said he would take more, as arranged, but urged Vincent to pay greater attention to commercial requirements. His nephew's wrath may be imagined. Mauve gave the finishing touch to it. For when the latter finally consented to inspect Vincent's work, he brutally indicated that he now considered Tersteeg and Cornelius to have acted mainly out of charity. But Vincent, so far from being discouraged and losing faith in himself, rejected Mauve's strictures with contempt and continued to work as hard as ever. He might be penniless. He might starve sometimes. But he would never descend to the 'manufacture of trivialities'.

But it was not only his typical artist's independence which put his 'patrons', the merchants and painters of The Hague, against him. They hated to think of such a failure dishonouring the name

SORROW, LITHOGRAPH. NOVEMBER 1885. V. W. VAN GOGH
COLLECTION, LAREN

'I have to listen to her gossip, as I'm with her all the time, but I don't worry about that. I've never had so much help as from this ugly[—]and faded creature. For me she's beautiful and I find in her exactly what I need. Life has marched over her body. Pain and visitations have marked it. Now I can get something out of it.'

Letter to van Rappard

he bore by the scandal of his private life. For he had decided to throw in his lot with Christine—Sien, as he called her—and to restore her to a decent way of life. Theo was convinced that she was unscrupulous and incapable of fidelity. But Vincent, completely absorbed in his charitable enthusiasm, took no notice of his brother's warnings. On the 7th June 1882 he had to go into hospital to be treated for gonorrhoea. He does not accuse Sien of having infected him. But it was undoubtedly she who was responsible for the twenty-three unpleasant days he spent in The Hague hospital. When he returned, he found she had given birth to a son. She already had another child, a sickly little girl afflicted with rickets. Vincent took all three of them into his lodgings. At last he had a family, a home. But he had no means of supporting it. The cost could not be met from his sole source of income, Theo's scanty contributions. Moreover, his association with this worthless creature had alienated everyone he knew. But he cared nothing for his poverty, degradation and disgrace. He had not the heart to abandon such unfortunate beings. And, after all, were not a wife and children the realisation of his dream? Surely it was 'better to live with a wretched prostitute than alone'. He meant to keep her, to marry her, to defy the moralists, conventional uncles and commercially-minded artists, to execute, in spite of all, the work which it was his destiny to accomplish. His letters at this period are defiant but also defensive. For Vincent considered himself bound to account for his behaviour to the brother who gave him both material and moral support. His explanations are always characterised by entire sincerity and frankness. Theo went on helping him. For he knew very well that to leave Vincent to his fate would be to 'sign his death-warrant'. Nevertheless, after a year of life with Sien, Vincent could not help feeling utterly worn out. Sien could not understand him. She neglected her children and thought of nothing but money. When at last, hopelessly in debt and exhausted by privation, he was obliged to call Theo to his assistance, she had already left him. She had gone back to prostitution and he himself was about to leave The Hague.

SUCH was the end of this two year period, the most important,

LE MOULIN DE LA GALETTE. 1886. MUSEO NACIONAL DE BELLAS ARTES, BUENOS AIRES.

together with that at Arles, of his life. It was at The Hague that Vincent became aware of the kind of man he was and of his vocation. It was at The Hague that he shook off the fetters of his education and foresaw his future. There can be no doubt that when he left the Dutch capital in September 1883 he was no longer the man he had been when he arrived there on the 31st December 1881.

THE WEAVER. FEBRUARY 1884. V. W. VAN GOGH COLLECTION, LAREN
'I feel much sympathy for them [the charcoal-burners and weavers] and should think myself happy if I could draw such characters in such a way as to make them known to a public hitherto practically unaware of them.

'The charcoal-burner is the man from the depths, de profundis; *the other, who looks so dreamy, almost meditative, almost like a sleep-walker, is the weaver.'*   Letter to Theo

He had completed his study of the human race and formed his opinion of it. His family, his colleagues, society at large, all those committed to received opinion, their morality and their habits, a whole world of irresponsibility and lies, what Heidegger was so rightly to call the world of 'one', of 'people', had grown hateful to Vincent. 'I abjure it all', he wrote to Theo. 'I am deserting the class into which I was born.' It was no matter if he should be thought a desperado, a fanatic, a 'misfit', for that was what he thought himself to be. He was so stern a critic of himself that there is no need for us to blame him. But although he had no pity on himself and never ceased to confess his weaknesses, he never ceased, either, to proclaim what he believed to be true. Even if the whole world cries 'Shame!' we are not necessarily bound to feel ashamed. As the Latin aphorism has it, we are not ashamed because we ought to be. (*Non pudet quia pudendum est.*)

Vincent had renounced the world and become an individual. He possessed an individual's dignity and virtues. He took responsibility for all his actions, struggled against the menace of extinction, took full advantage of the self with which he had been endowed, despised compromise and facile achievements, recognised the continual presence of anguish and death and showed that he cared nothing for this world's goods and the worship of money. For such a being cordial, open-hearted and loving his neighbour as himself—a point on which I should like to insist—solitude could

CALENDERING. NUENEN.
KRÖLLER-MÜLLER RIJKSMUSEUM, OTTERLO

be nothing but the worst of evils. It was not Vincent who left his family. It was his family which practically turned him out. The advances he made to other painters were rejected, intelligibly enough in view of their egotism, self-conceit and jealousy. He did all he could to acquire friends. But he was friendless. His father, his uncles, his colleagues, God's own pastors and even God Himself eluded his attempts to approach them. When he overflowed with tender and trustful affection, he was told to be reasonable. When he innocently laid claim to the free exercise of his faculties, objections were raised on the score of respect for convention and moral law. But he loved truth too much to join practical people in their reliance on the comforting foundations of morality and logic. It was not Vincent's way to be lost in admiration before a cathedral and meditate upon man's ultimate destination. It was in the tired face of a miner, the wrinkled brow of a peasant woman or 'the eyes of a little child waking' that he believed he could see 'something deeper, more immeasurable and more lasting than the ocean'. He did not draw his strength from such principles or abstractions as ordinary men are in the habit of invoking to preserve them from grief and anxiety. It was for reality, with its joys, its elements of security and its tranquil hours, but also and especially with its sudden apprehensions and horrors, that Vincent cared. It was there that he felt himself obliged to live.

The 'reality' of Vincent, so unlike that of other people, yet none the less real for not being ordinary, was the source of all his raptures and torments. At times he was exalted, at times depressed by it. But he never submitted tamely to its influence. His attitude was not that of a stoic or ascetic. On the contrary, he was a rebel and a fighter, with a fierce determination to overcome adversity, sickness and poverty and triumph over hypocrisy and misunderstanding, to the very end of his endurance. As a 'realist', he had a deep sense of communal solidarity. Consequently, nothing pained him more than the distrust and hostility of others. He would have enjoyed 'real life', i.e. living like other men. But he was not like other men.

In giving shelter to that wretched woman and her two children he believed he had made a home for himself. He took a puerile pride

VIEW OF INDUSTRIAL TOWN. 1887. STEDELIJK MUSEUM, AMSTERDAM.

in endowing his miserable dwelling with all the splendours of his heart and soul. There can be no doubt, moreover, that the presence of those three beings stimulated his energy. His confidential letters to Theo at that time are full of determination, faith and hope. The intense concentration with which he worked refreshed and animated him to an extent which, perhaps, he was never to enjoy again. His break with convention was still quite recent. He seems to have been intoxicated by the prospects it had opened up for him. At that moment he had completely seen through the pretences and frauds of a decadent world. He did not intend to be a slave to routine, material possessions and prejudices, like one of those typical Calvinist citizens whom he despised. He meant to be a free, responsible, forward-looking being, one who would succeed only by surpassing himself. Towards his thirtieth year he had become

49

aware of a process of conversion similar to Kierkegaard's, which the latter had called 'the great earthquake'. The destinies of the Dutch painter and the Danish thinker have in fact so much in common that we may well be justified in supposing that Vincent, if he had not been so highly an individual character of flesh and blood and found an outlet for his genius in art, might now have been revered as a philosopher.

In August 1881 he painted his first canvases, notably the *Still Life with Jug* (Cat. 7), and at the same time made a start with water-colour and lithography. But he continued to feel happiest in drawing. He would set out at dawn, pencil in hand, for the Scheveningen fish-curing yards (p. 22) or the more crowded streets of The Hague. He also drew the sheds and shipyards he could see from his window and the distorted shapes of trees (p. 21). Some thirty of his figures are derived from aged male patients at the hospital (pp. 26, 220). He made rapid progress and knew it, though he noticed 'errors and omissions' in his sketches. He adds: 'I am hopeful, brother. In a few years' time, or even any day now, you may be able to examine work by me which will give you some pleasure after all the trouble you have taken on my behalf.' Further on in the same letter he writes: 'What am I, according to most people? They think me negligible, a queer, disagreeable fellow, with no social position and never likely to have one. . . . I should like to prove by my work that there is something, all the same, in the heart of this queer, perfectly negligible fellow.' How well he knew himself and how well he could express what he felt! A few days later he wrote: 'I feel great creative power within me and I know that a day will come when I shall be in a position to produce good things regularly, day after day.'

There were already good, very good, things in the work he was doing with such lucidity and passion at that time. There were landscapes of wide perspectives, figures vigorously posed, a correct distribution of light and shade and an assured line. But the style was still too laboured, in the fashion of the British draughtsmen by whom Vincent was influenced at this period. He began to collect the drawings of Gavarni, Millet, de Groux and Gustave Doré, preferring them to his Dutch contemporaries, whose little tricks he could easily detect. He read with unflagging interest the biographies of the Barbizon painters and bore their recommendations and aphorisms in mind. He often visited the royal museum, the Mauritshuis, to admire pictures by Rembrandt, Hals and Ruysdael. From dawn till dusk, in all sorts of weather, he drew in the crowded slums of Geest and Slijkeinde or in the sand-dunes on the coast. He was so anxious to learn that he contrived to study the art of both Dutch and foreign masters, while at the same time reading great writers such as Victor Hugo, Michalet, Balzac, Zola, Daudet and Dickens and keeping up a regular correspondence with Theo and van Rappard. And when he returned home, exhausted, in the evening, it was to contend with yet more anxieties and toil, a sick wife and neglected children.

Vigorous as he was both physically and morally, he sometimes faltered. 'I've been feeling ill these last few days . . . one longs for a visit from a friend at such times.' For privations and overwork worried him less than his isolation. His enforced admission to hospital seems to have undermined his resolution. On that occasion he wrote to Theo: 'People like myself ought not to be ill . . . art is a jealous suitor, who won't be cut out by illness.' He had scarcely returned home, still in pain, before he picked up his brush again. 'I live for painting in the first place and only secondarily to keep well.' The prophetic lines follow: 'I believe I am justified in concluding, without exaggeration, that physically I shall be able to stand this life, in spite of all, for a few more years, let's say from six to ten. I'm not going to take any care of myself or avoid excitement and worry; it's a matter of relative indifference to me how long I live . . . so I am living like an ignoramus who only knows one thing for certain: I must accomplish the work I have set myself to do in a few years . . . the world is of hardly any importance to me, except for the fact that I owe it something, which I am morally bound to pay, since I have been wandering about in it for so many years and ought to show my gratitude by bequeathing it a few mementoes in the shape of drawings or pictures not undertaken to please any particular tendency but to express sincere human feeling.'

The period which Vincent allowed himself, in making this

testamentary statement, for accomplishing his work and retaining enough strength to do it was eventually ratified by Fate. He had mentioned six to ten years. He died seven years later.

In September 1883, after parting from Sien, he left for the province of Drenthe in the north-eastern Netherlands. By that time he had much to boast of. Though he had begun to draw in 1879, it was during the twenty-two months he spent at The Hague that he definitely decided, of his own free will, what he was going to do.

His case, accordingly, was that of a man who, though he felt capable of living like other people, could nevertheless make his own plans and create his own personality by overcoming his weaknesses and surpassing himself, so as to render the talents he possessed an essential part of his nature. He had decided to become an artist—in other words, the only kind of person whose calling is due to an operation of Destiny, a decree of Providence, a summons from the absolute nature of things. There can hardly be any other example of such a victory by the mysterious power of conscience, by an individual in search of himself over the edict of superhuman authority.

It was at The Hague that Vincent served his true apprenticeship, deepened his insight and trained his hand. He lost no time over it. For he was able to discriminate at once between good and bad influences, to reject dictation which could only do him harm, while accepting such advice as was beneficial. When Mauve instructed him to use charcoal for drawing, he at first obeyed. But afterwards he abandoned this method and returned to his hard carpenter's pencil, with which he obtained better results. When his brother recommended the use of chalk, he took to it with success and persevered enthusiastically with that medium. He was attracted by every kind of practice and technique—printers' ink, water-colour, oils and even lithography. One of his prints, unquestion-ably the most successful, is to-day celebrated. He himself entitled it, in English, *Sorrow* (p. 43). It was executed in November 1882 after a number of sketches for which Sien was the model. At that time he was engaged on a series of female figures illustrating affliction (Cat. 12), and stressing the toilworn aspect of his peasants and people drinking, as in the case of the seated elderly

FLOWERS IN BLUE VASE. 1887. KRÖLLER-MÜLLER RIJKSMUSEUM, OTTERLO.

labourer represented with his elbows on his knees and his face buried in his hands (p. 220). He returned to this subject at St. Remy in 1890 with the painting entitled *On the Threshold of Eternity.* Everything he did at this period expressed grief, poverty, irremediable melancholy and the pitiable condition of labourers, helpless old men, deserted women and orphans.

Vincent had made a few timid attempts at oil-painting while at Etten in 1881. But it was not until the summer of 1882 that he took it up seriously, probably urged by Theo, who had come to see him at The Hague. With the money given him by his brother he bought brushes, tubes of colour and an easel. He was soon expressing his enthusiasm for the medium. 'I've been toiling and moiling to such an extent that I was utterly exhausted after painting seven studies. . . . I feel ideas about colour coming to me as I paint, which I never had before. They're big and exciting.' A glow of exaltation sent him out to explore the roads, dunes and fields around The Hague. Nothing could restrain him. He was indifferent to cold, wind and rain. His models were fishermen, menders of nets, potato-gatherers, the coast at Scheveningen and trees (Cat. 10). He painted in all about a score of pictures, working feverishly, without intermission. Sometimes he lost his temper. But immediately afterwards he would try to find out what was wrong, for he knew that his technique was still rudimentary. Yet, though he was well aware of his limitations, he never doubted that he would overcome them with the aid of intelligence, energy and tenacity. As early as the 1st May 1881 he was writing: 'I wish everyone could have the faculty I am beginning to acquire of reading a book quickly and retaining a very clear impression of it. In reading, as in studying a picture, one has to be able to pick out the best at a glance, without hesitation, and be sure one's favourable judgment is correct.' He was to absorb with equal promptitude the science of the old masters and the dexterity of The Hague painters.

It is certain that so gifted a man, conscious of such high 'productive power', could not have been entirely unhappy, in spite of his destitution, his anxieties and the contempt with which he was regarded. And yet no man deserved contempt less. It must not be supposed that he wasted Theo's contributions on alcohol and tobacco. He used the money to buy books and a great quantity of prints, to pay for his clothes, his room and his periods in hospital, as well as for the food of his dependants. In addition to his very serious material difficulties, he experienced galling anxieties and cruel disappointments. Yet he was never heard to complain. In these utterly abject conditions he was conscious only of the 'gleam from on high' and the child in its cradle. He knew, moreover, that he could count on Theo, his indulgent and affectionate brother, who showed such constant solicitude for him, supporting and encouraging him, reviving his energy, defending him against his incensed family and protecting him from the disastrous consequences of his quarrels. It may be said, therefore, that when Vincent at last became convinced that Sien had 'fallen too low to rise again' and when he accordingly left The Hague for good, a period of relative happiness began for him.

Until December 1883 he remained in the province of Drenthe. It was a mournful land of plains, moors and moss, yet inexpressibly colourful, to an artist, in autumn. He tried, nevertheless, to grasp its elusive tones, painting certain pictures in twilight or on grey days, beneath a sky of infinite melancholy (Cat. 16). He had at once achieved intimacy with this desolate countryside, tramping over it from morning till night. But its rustic inhabitants were reserved and inhospitable. He soon began to feel stifled in this dismal environment, which lacked all human warmth. On the 1st December 1883 he fled for refuge to the parsonage at Nuenen in Brabant, where his father was now pastor.

We may assume that Vincent, in thus returning to his family, was making a further attempt at reconciliation. He was duly welcomed, but soon confronted again with the blank wall of misunderstanding which had originally alienated him. The pastor had not forgiven his association with Christine, his disputes with his uncles and his choice of a profession considered discreditable. There had been little change, furthermore, in Vincent's own manners. At thirty as at twenty, he was the same shaggy redhead as ever, clumsily built, abrupt in his movements, dressed anyhow and incapable of complying with domestic routine and the habits of decent society. When friends called, he was told to keep away

MONTMARTRE FÊTE. 1886-7. V. W. VAN GOGH COLLECTION, LAREN.

from the house. In 1957 the parsonage was entirely rebuilt. It had been a comfortable single-storied dwelling, surrounded by a garden. The lean-to barn can still be seen which Vincent had fitted up as an improvised studio and to which he returned after his long country walks (p. 30). But he felt he was there on sufferance. His pride revolted against the feeling. In January 1884 his mother broke a leg and he nursed her with exemplary patience and devotion. From that moment his ties with his family seemed to improve. He hoped for a definite reconciliation. But unfortunately a love-affair, once more prevented any such thing.

A neighbour named Margot Begemann had fallen in love with Vincent and he had proposed to her. In his astonishment at finding that anyone loved him, he had responded to her advances less from a similar feeling than out of pity. Though she was the older by ten years, the couple immediately planned to marry. But the woman's parents soon put a stop to the engagement and ordered the impudent dauber back to his brushes. Margot, in despair, took poison. But she recovered. Vincent, for his part, did not take long to forget the affair.

Meanwhile, life at the parsonage continued to be dismal and monotonous. The pastor and his son again began to quarrel. In the intervals of these disputes they avoided each other. Elizabeth, one of Vincent's sisters, later gave an account of the midday meals at the Nuenen parsonage. Her parents, her brother and her sisters sat at the table, while Vincent crouched in a corner with a plate on his knees, munching dry bread with one hand and shading his eyes with the other, so as to get a better idea of the effect of a drawing or painting placed beside him on a chair. These simultaneous occupations kept him out of the general conversation. But if the talk turned to literature he would suddenly break his silence, only to return to it a moment afterwards. He was like a dog, irritating everybody. 'A dog understands', he wrote to Theo, 'that it is only kept in the house on sufferance. So it naturally tries to find a resting-place elsewhere.' He could not get used to the humiliations inflicted on him. He grew more and more touchy, eventually interpreting any 'little favours' shown him as so many veiled insults. The villagers considered him an eccentric failure, a

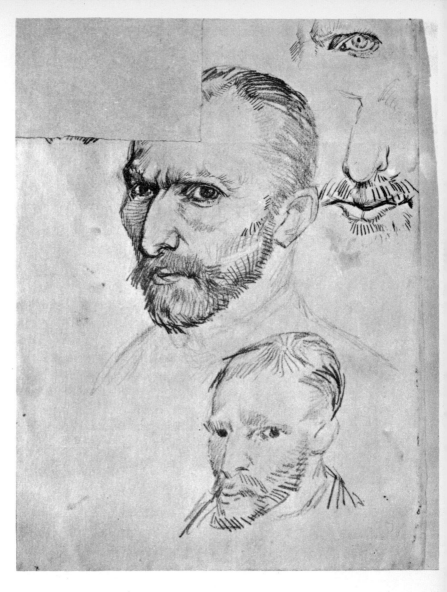

SELF-PORTRAIT. SKETCH. 1886-1887. V. W. VAN GOGH COLLECTION,
LAREN

'*I feel a strength within me that I must develop, a fire I can't put out, but must
stir up, though I don't know where it will lead me and I shouldn't be surprised
if it brought me to a bad end. . . . In certain situations it's better to be conquered
than conqueror, more Prometheus than Jupiter.*'
Letter to Theo

good-for-nothing. Middle-class families kept out of his way. But he did make a few friends among the lowest social groups, peasants and women employed in weeding and cotton-spinning, textile workers. He used them as models (Cat. 17, 19, 20). They often appear in his paintings and drawings, either at work in the fields or in some humble room, dimly lit from a narrow window, through which a glimpse is caught of pallid sky or a patch of landscape. He was in the habit of setting up his easel, accompanied by an amateur painter, the tanner Kerssemakers, on the outskirts of Nuenen, to sketch a water-mill, an old tower, a thatched cottage (Cat. 35) or an ox-cart (Cat. 21), surrounded by toiling farm-labourers and women digging or harvesting potatoes or else carrying wood home on snowy days (Cat. 22). He made many striking portraits of rugged peasant women. Their features under the characteristic Brabant headdress, express a boorish truculence in the snub noses, high cheek-bones, prominent eyeballs and square-cut chins (Cat. 29, 31, 32, 33, 37). In seated figures he dwells lovingly on the calloused, chapped hands, distorted by strenuous agricultural labour.

Vincent also executed numerous still-life paintings, as of an open bible, a hat, a beer-jug, a copper frying-pan, a tobacco-jar, bottles (Cat. 25), a pair of clogs, fruit, potatoes (Cat. 38, 41) and birds' nests. We may also follow him into the homes of the Nuenen craftsmen and peasants, where we may find a blacksmith or a basket-maker at work, or a housewife darning, grinding coffee, peeling vegetables, sweeping (Cat. 30) or scouring a saucepan. A man may be smoking his pipe (Cat. 26), having a meal, or simply seated in meditation, looking at nothing in particular, on a bench (Cat. 28). Vincent found something worth drawing or painting in everything he saw. He wished to train his hand to meet every technical demand and to familiarise himself with every style and every kind of material. He did not care whether he painted in oils on canvas or on panels. He drew either with blacklead, charcoal or ink, or simultaneously with black and coloured pencils and with chalk and charcoal. He turned from wash drawing to water-colour and from water-colour to gouache, sometimes employing several of these media in the same work.

CORNFIELD WITH LARK. 1887. V. W. VAN GOGH COLLECTION, LAREN.

In ink-drawings he would use a brush or even a reed-pen as readily as a nib. For he had decided about this time to employ the stems, first shaping them for the purpose, of reeds from the marshes, with a view to strengthening his line. He resorted to this expedient, for example, in combination with black lead and white chalk, in his *Peasant Digging*. Nor had he given up lithography, as is proved by the engraving entitled *Peasant Man and Women in the Fields* and the print of the *Potato Eaters* which brought about his break with van Rappard.

Vincent's works during the two years he lived at Nuenen reveal something better than promise behind their imperfections. They

61

have the confidence of youth and a marked originality. He is certainly reminiscent of Millet in the figures of his peasants bowed over the soil. But Millet never achieved such vivacity of expression, so summary and bold a presentation. Again, Vincent's admirable studies of trees recall those of Georges Michel, though the French landscape painter seems insipid in comparison with the Dutchman. His thatched cottages may also be thought to bear some relation to those of Rembrandt, the free and robust treatment of his figures to that typical of Franz Hals and, still more, of Delacroix. Yet in spite of these affinities it is undeniable that Vincent's personality had a definite character of its own. In any case, though he lacked the experience and cunning of the contemporary artists in Holland, he surpassed them in sincerity, energy, acuteness of observation and in the sober, deeply evocative rhythms of his style. None of the 'masters' of The Hague, whether Jacob Maris, Mauve or Israels, could have painted such canvases as the *Weaver* (Cat. 20), the *Autumn Landscape* (Cat. 44), a still-life such as the *Bible* (Cat. 42) or a scene such as the *Potato Eaters* (Cat. 41). We need do no more than compare these four pictures with those of his Dutch contemporaries who still remained bound to the academic conventions of the day in order to appreciate the novelty of Van Gogh's highly promising contribution to painting at this early date of his career.

Looking back to-day at the whole body of his work in the 'Dutch period', between December 1881 and November 1885, we may well agree in calling it his 'sombre period', in contrast with the 'bright' period of Paris and Arles. Both subjects and style are sombre and naturalistic. Yet he was already taking liberties with reality, sacrificing detail, emphasising mass, reducing the significance of form in one place and accentuating it to the verge of caricature in another, so that his countrymen used as they were to classical refinement, must have been greatly surprised by his portraits of men and women with round eyes, flat noses, projecting ears and gross features. He heard himself called sordid and coarse. But he was not afraid of exposing himself to insults of that kind. Was he supposed to give 'a conventional polish to pictures of peasants'? They ought, on the contrary, to 'reek of the kitchen'.

But were these pictures quite so sombre as he and others said they were? Consider the *Weaver* of May 1884. It is true that only browns and greys are employed. But the interior represented is bathed in silvery light. And though the air does not seem at all rarefied it is transparently bright and clear. Or we may turn to the picture called *Roofs* (p. 13). The workmanship is most delicate, with meticulous detail and a fine gloss, quite devoid of heaviness, vulgarity and aggressive intention. The style of the *Girl in the Forest,* painted three months later, in September 1882, is incontestably less laboured, broader in treatment and more vigorous. The touch is freer, the paint richer and thicker. The *Autumn Landscape* (Cat. 44) of 1885, with the ochre foliage of its trees, the soft green of its grass and the pinks and pale blues of its sky, conveys excellently the gentle melancholy of the dying year. Finally, the most typical work of Vincent's 'sombre' period and the most important of his pictures of peasants, the *Potato Eaters,* was executed, and often revised, in 1885.

Of this subject a study in black chalk, two drawings, a lithograph and three paintings are known. The first of the latter is a small canvas bearing the signs of haste and representing four persons only. The third version, in the V. W. van Gogh collection, is decidedly inferior to the second, which summarises, though considered by Vincent a preliminary work, the results of the innumerable drawings and paintings in which the artist dealt with the inhabitants of Brabant. This picture belongs to the Kröller-Müller Museum. It represents an interior with a family of peasants seated round a plate of potatoes. The woman wearing a white bonnet, seen in profile on the right, is pouring coffee from a pot into a cup. Beside her a man is raising another cup to his lips. To the woman's left a girl with her back to the light and the spectator is flanked by a peasant wearing a bluish-green cap, a blue blouse and brown trousers. He is thrusting a fork into one of the potatoes in the smoking plate on the table, which is covered with a white cloth. On the man's left another woman, with a large white headdress, facing the spectator, is doing the same thing. A shaded oil-lamp hangs from the ceiling.

However rapid the execution of this picture may have been, it seems to have required considerable thought beforehand. Vincent confirms this supposition with the remark: 'It took me the whole winter to work out the heads and hands.' The four people are logically arranged in a circle under the soft light of the lamp. They are sturdily built and securely seated on their chairs. Their arms are solidly attached to their trunks and the caps of the two women are perfectly adjusted to the shapes of their heads. The powerful physique of the figures, with their gnarled hands and bony faces, suggests the harshness of their lives. In the halo of light cast by the lamp swifter and heavier brush-strokes indicate the brighter passages and at the same time define form. The composition is firmly balanced. Tones are harmoniously organised and volumes vigorously denoted. The planes are well distributed and accurately related to one another. The canvas has great interest, though weaknesses can be detected in it. Bodily structure is not sufficiently evident beneath the clothing. The painting is weighed down by its deep shadows. Contrasts seem a little facile and simplifications sometimes crude. Lastly, the style is impaired by the sentimentality of the intention behind it. But when van Rappard calls a work which he only knew from Vincent's lithograph of it 'not serious', he merely convicts himself of misunderstanding the picture or prejudice against it. It is no wonder that Vincent strongly objected to this criticism. As for the emphasis of the brush-strokes, the accentuation and distortion for which he was blamed, some critics have asserted that he did not adopt this style for plastic reasons, but to express the affection and pity he felt for his models. 'I have tried', he wrote to Theo on the subject of this picture,' to give it as natural an air as the people themselves have when they eat their potatoes by lamplight with the very hands they use to work the soil. . . . I wished to suggest by it an entirely different manner of life from that to which we civilised persons are accustomed.'

It is to be regretted that the critics referred to only quoted this statement in support of a mistaken theory. It is absurd to suppose that Vincent was unaffected by plastic considerations. He was writing at the same time to van Rappard: 'I have painted a certain number of heads and drawn several figures of peasants, men digging and women weeding and reaping. In so doing I was

PORTRAIT OF THE ARTIST. 1887. V. W. VAN GOGH COLLECTION, LAREN

concerned, directly or indirectly, with the main problem, that of colour. I am aware that certain colours are complementary, such as red and green, blue and orange, yellow and violet. Their regular association and reciprocal influence are as evident in nature as is light and shade. Another question with which I am daily concerned is the very one which you state, erroneously in my view, that I neglect. I mean the reproduction of form in its *relief,* main outlines and mass. Here it is not primarily, but only ultimately, that *contour* has to be considered.'

In the same letter, written in September 1885, he explains his aims in the *Potato Eaters*. He wanted to show the 'peculiar effect of light' in a squalid cottage, with dark colours 'counterbalancing' brighter passages. Any neglect of torso conformation had been due to his excessive concentration on colour organisation. On the other hand he had drawn the heads and hands with great care, these details being more important than any others. He, too, could see the faults of the picture. But he immediately adds that he sometimes deliberately fell short of accuracy and perfection in his renderings and had 'good grounds' for doing so. Such short-comings are not permitted by the realist school, which always criticises them, the realist substituting mere dexterity for creative intention.

The academically trained van Rappard had laid down restrictive rules from which van Gogh, in his new self-confidence, had freed himself. He retorted to van Rappard's criticisms: 'What I have to say is simply this: the correct drawing of a figure according to academic formulae, with uniform and meticulous brushwork, does not adequately meet the imperative requirements of pictorial art in in modern times.' One can hear the very voice of an artist of to-day in this protest. Yet van Gogh had only been painting for four years and had never yet seen an impressionist picture. He was particularly hurt to find his friend resorting to the same old story which had been so spitefully dinned into his ears by his family, by the dealers and people like Tersteeg, Cornelius, Mauve and Goupil. But he was no longer anxious for advice and approval. He himself knew what he was doing and what he was capable of doing. No doubt, so far as he personally was concerned, he was 'doomed to

THE TERRACE OF THE TUILERIES, PARIS. V. W. VAN GOGH COLLECTION, LAREN

bleak poverty. But that prospect encourages rather than depresses me and may even increase my powers of work. Don't suppose that you are the only person to believe or ever to have believed it a duty to criticise me to the point of crushing me out of existence, with the result that I am in the state you know. On the contrary, something very like this has always been my lot, so far.'

These phrases in the letter, one of capital importance, that broke off Vincent's relations with van Rappard, cannot be misinterpreted. Vincent is speaking here as a forerunner, a revolutionary artist announcing the art of the future. The uncompromising nature of his statements, the clarity of his thought, the generosity behind it and the ardour of his conviction are most admirable. At the end of the Nuenen period everything in his writings and in his works proves his full self-consciousness, both of the immense potentialities his personality offered and his ability to realise them. That he was still under the spell of naturalism cannot be disputed. He might take liberties with it. But he was none the less too deeply committed to it to emancipate himself without delay. His tastes and

THE GARDENS OF THE TUILERIES. V. W. VAN GOGH COLLECTION, LAREN

ideas, after all, had been formed in an environment traditionally respectful of the real, or at any rate of the appearances of reality. But we may note that a change was beginning to take place in him. Theo at least was well aware of it.

Theo was living in Paris, in the thick of the impressionist movement. In his view the popular style of painting, with which Vincent was infatuated, the sombre or gloomy depiction of peasants, had gone out of date and been far surpassed by the achievements of those who painted light. As against Rembrandt, Lhermitte, de Groux, Millet and the Barbizon painters so much admired by Vincent, his brother extolled the works of Daumier, Manet, Claude Monet and Pissarro. It had not even occurred to Vincent that a painter could do without brown, Prussian blue and bituminous black. Were they not the colours of the earth and those who dwelt close to it? But Theo preferred the pure colours used by the new generation. His arguments imperceptibly gained ground with Vincent, though the latter vehemently opposed them. They were helped by his reading, for he was always avid of knowledge. It was at this time that he began to revere Delacroix, the forerunner of impressionism. Vincent was led to reflect on a strange observation by that master, to the effect that such great colourists as Titian, Velasquez, Vermeer and Rubens took no notice of the rule about local colour. At first disconcerted by what was to Vincent the novelty of this remark he came across its again in a book by Gigoux, where it was explained and justified by the statement that complementary colours, when juxtaposed, cause light to vibrate, whereas, when mixed, they destroy it. Vincent was further agitated by a passage in the book of the Goncourts on Chardin. 'On reading it', he writes, 'I thought of Vermeer of Delft in his Hague landscape. On a close scrutiny—it's quite incredible—the colours are found to be altogether different from those which are apparent at a distance.' He went on to read Charles Blanc, who had called attention, from 1880 onwards, to a painting by Delacroix in which, by green hatching on pink flesh, 'the artist obtains a result which is precisely that known as dazzling'.

He was reluctantly beginning to doubt the necessity of local colour. He wrote to Theo: 'By not using local colour am I to understand anything so drastic as approval of a painter who distributes colours mixed on his palette instead of those provided by nature? I can't deny that for years I have devoted myself, almost in vain and with painful results, to the study of nature, the struggle with reality. I shouldn't care not to have made that "mistake".' He wondered whether he had given himself all that trouble for nothing. At any rate it seems that his argument with Theo and also some of the books he read eventually made him thoroughly uneasy. Had he been wrong? Were his convictions nothing but a set of aberrations? He was morally tormented by such questions. They had to be answered if his life were to have any meaning.

The events in Vincent's life have been attentively studied and regarded as of great importance. But his artistic development has been neglected, though its transformations, less evident and more secretly conducted than his wanderings, contributed no less to the fabric of his personality. Neither the education, the character, the mentality nor the physical sufferings of van Gogh, nor his relations with others and with his time, nor the picturesque episodes in his life, suffice to explain his work. Its exceptional quality has inspired an army of biographers, novelists, psychologists, psychiatrists and interpreters of all descriptions. Yet none or very few have paid attention to the specifically aesthetic and perfectly deliberate research from which his work proceeded. It was not an instinctive, spontaneous creation of genius stimulated by a touch of madness. For genius in its primary condition, before it is consolidated by long and patient labour, has never produced any lasting effect. Nor is van Gogh's work simply the outcome of a docile apprenticeship, the learning of technical formulae and prescriptions. It was prepared by a series of experiences and reflections, doubts and convictions, sometimes by direct intuition, but above all by decisions of the intellect.

It is questionable whether a hundred 'Passionate Lives' of van Gogh or another hundred 'Tragic Lives' of him would bring us any nearer to understanding his art. And yet how little of himself he hides, how clearly he maps out in his correspondence the road he followed with his train of afflictions, torments, disappointments, persevering efforts, sudden shifts of direction and exhausting conflicts! It is here that we must look for the real story of van Gogh, if we are not to regard him solely as a romantic hero, but as the creator of work impressive on its own account alone, work which revealed new horizons of the potentialities of colour to the modern painter.

For although Vincent's pictures were still gloomy, he was already beginning to be obsessed by the problem of colour. When he exclaims, 'Yes, these studies of mine are altogether too dark and dismal! And yet, what about the blacks in Franz Hals, Rembrandt and Velasquez? To me shadows seem definitely dull, if not black. Can I be wrong?' it is the Dutch realist, the painter of peasants, who is talking. It is the innovator who admits, immediately afterwards, that in his opinion the first and most important problem a painter has to decide is that of complementary colours in juxtaposition. He daily grows more and more absorbed in studying the laws of colour. 'If only we had been taught them when we were young! But it is as though fate had decreed that the search for light must be a long one in most people's lives.' Light! That was the operative word. Henceforward Vincent was to concentrate upon it. He went far in quest of it, drawing nearer and nearer

PÈRE TANGUY. V. W. VAN GOGH COLLECTION, LAREN

its burning centre, at the risk of himself perishing there. He bent his whole mind and will to the subject. The most intense of his pleasures and pains were derived from it. It was of light he was thinking when, on leaving for Antwerp, he wrote: 'I am violently anxious to see Rubens.' Rubens, in fact, was one of the master-colourists invoked by Delacroix.

MONTMARTRE GARDENS IN WINTER. 1887. V. W. VAN GOGH COLLECTION, LAREN

On the 27th March 1885 the pastor died suddenly. Although Vincent had voluntarily renounced his share of the family inheritance, he was bound to realise that his relations with the Nuenen household had hardly improved, while those he maintained with the village had grown even worse. An artist of thirty-two who never sells a picture, never goes to mass, rambles about the countryside in rags like a tramp and consorts with the riffraff of the population can only be thought a black sheep. Out of doors as at home, he felt that he was being regarded, more than ever, as an intruder. His only refuge from these conditions was work, his only consolation the writing of those querulous, indignant and exclamatory letters to Theo. But the latter warned him that he would find himself completely alone one day if he did not change his behaviour. Vincent answered: 'I refuse to believe that I deserve such a thing. I'm sure that nothing I have ever done or ever shall do could deprive me of the right to consider myself a normal human being.' He becomes nervous and depressed, sickened by every obstacle to his desire to communicate with others. Sometimes he proclaims his sympathy for the French revolutionaries and the rioters of 1848 and his solidarity with them. As formerly at The Hague and later at Arles, he wanted desperately to work with other painters. He loathed his solitude. No sage ever did more to seek it out than he did to escape from it. The widow of the Catholic sexton from whom he had hired a couple of rooms so as to avoid the constant disputes with his family describes him as a good, simple man who was never sulky and worked incessantly, even at night, by the niggardly flame of a single candle. We are accordingly justified in wondering whether ordinary citizens did not themselves arbitrarily invent the account they gave of him as a refractory and abnormal being and whether the refractoriness and abnormality which he eventually did show were not the fatal consequences of the guilt of society. For the curtain has not yet gone up on the last act of the tragedy.

We may almost say that Vincent was evicted from Nuenen. The parish priest forbade his flock to pose for the painter, who could do nothing without models. One dark November morning he took the train for Antwerp. He left with his feelings unrecognised and

BOAT AT ASNIÈRES. V. W. VAN GOGH COLLECTION, LAREN

dissatisfied, in the hope of returning one day. But he never saw his country again.

H<small>E</small> reached Antwerp on the 28th November 1885 and at once rented a room at 194 Beeldekensstraat. He was interested and stimulated by the novelty of streets full of movement, and the swarming life of the harbour of the great city, above all by the sailors, dock labourers and girls he saw about. He drew the cathedral, the castle of Steen, a row of old houses, a square and the heads of Flemish men and women (Cat. 47). He had gained self-confidence now and was less troubled by technical rules. He represents, for example, in *The Wharf*, painted on a dark winter's day, a sky of pouring rain hatched in with rapid brush-strokes, a muddy pavement with a few pedestrians outlined in black and some steamers with smoke coming from the funnels. The whole scene is bathed in a diffused violet light, cut by the whitish streak of the Scheldt. It is a dashing piece of work, built up by the organisation of masses from a single flow of colour.

Whenever he stopped drawing or painting he visited churches and museums. He did not admire Rubens without qualification, considering him superficial. But he 'exulted in the *Descent from the Cross* because here the painter does really try to express and represent with truth—however insubstantial his figures may some-times be—an atmosphere, through colour combination of joy, serenity and grief'. At the docks he bought a batch of Japanese paintings on silk brought back by seamen from the Far East. It is doubtful, however, whether he knew that the Goncourts had made such things fashionable in Paris. He decorated his room with them and spent hours studying them. With his imagination aflame, he saw Antwerp in the guise of a 'great Japanese work of art, weird, original and unprecedented in style'. These prints, with their clear contours, unshaded light and pure colours laid on with no attention to gradations of tone, put the finishing touch to his conversion.

It was actually at this time that Vincent really found his true direction. His dark manner, his pictures of peasants, the realistic style to which he had been so much attached that he had taken

THE ARLES COUNTRY UNDER SNOW. FEBRUARY-MARCH 1888. COLLECTION
OF MR. AND MRS. JUSTIN K. THANNHAUSER, NEW YORK
*'I must tell you that at the first fall the snow was almost two feet deep every-
where. It's still falling . . . I've seen magnificent red vineyards, backed by mountains of the subtlest lilac. The snow-scenes, with their white peaks as luminous
as the snow itself, were very like the winter landscapes painted by the Japanese.'*
Letter to Theo

great trouble over it, began to lose its hold on him. Though still
not quite sure what he wanted, he became vaguely aware of an
avenue towards a new world of clarity, bliss and truth, a new
conception of man's relations with nature, a naturalism of so con-
templative and spiritualised a character that his own naturalism
came to seem to him both vulgar and unduly restricted. He understood better than any of his contemporaries what the Japanese

77

masters had to teach. He was later to mention it often and think continually of it. From Arles, he was to write to Theo: 'In studying Japanese art one finds out how the wise, the philosophic, the intelligent man spends his time. He spends it studying a single blade of grass ... well, aren't the Japanese teaching us true religion then? They live in nature as if they themselves were flowers.' His palette was already growing brighter. Nevertheless, though he was glad to learn from the Japanese, appreciated their restraint and envied their animation and serenity, he was quite incapable of being like them. The endless lack of money, overwork and the permanent injury to his health all contributed to the aggravation of his anguish and melancholy.

In the daytime, when not working at a particular subject, he attended courses at the Municipal Academy. From eight till ten in the evenings he practised drawing from life at a class in the Grand Marché. From ten until midnight he went to another life-class in Reynders Street. For all this activity he needed expensive materials which he bought with the necessarily limited funds provided by his brother Theo. Being thus faced with the choice between working and satisfying his hunger, he was condemned to exhausting under-nourishment. He lived exclusively on bread, a little cheese and coffee. Consequently, he was in a perpetual state of weakness. He suffered from internal pains, lost about ten of his teeth and coughed incessantly. One day, when he was feeling ill, he could no longer hide the truth from Theo: 'I must tell you that I am literally starving.' His distress suggested macabre subjects to him, such as *The Skull with a Cigarette*, and an astonishing little drawing entitled *Hanging Skeleton*. He also painted two self-portraits in oils at this time, in which he appears smoking a pipe (Cat. 46). They were the first of many that are landmarks in his career, the features expressing unfathomable depths of melancholy and a profound disenchantment, as though desire had already withered in the man. One of his fellow-pupils at the Municipal Academy describes him as having 'an angular physiognomy, with a pointed nose and a short pipe planted in the middle of a bristling, unkempt beard.' He painted himself just like that. His negligent dress, abrupt manners and astounding rapidity at work rendered him unpopular

THE FOOTPATH. MARCH 1888. V. W. VAN GOGH COLLECTION, LAREN

with such teachers and pupils as would otherwise have made advances to him. Nor did he, unfortunately, ever conceal his hostility to academic instruction, which he rightly considered pernicious: 'To tell the truth, I find all the drawings I see to be positively bad, absurd failures. I know very well that my own are utterly different. Time will tell who is aiming in the right direction.' The teachers often called this perverse pupil to order. At last Vincent could stand their criticisms no longer. He left Antwerp suddenly, for Paris, where he arrived on the 28th February 1886.

HE was now thirty-three. Freed from his religious, moral and humanitarian obsessions and from the meticulously naturalistic tradition that was choking the growth of Dutch art, he had realised the inadequacy of his sombre pictures of peasants and was

79

ready to be influenced by French taste, by the French sense of order and proportion, open-mindedness and affability. After this date he talked and wrote only in French, using the language in an awkward, harsh style, sprinkled with incorrect expressions, but also on occasion, owing to his intense preoccupation with sincerity, magnificently phrased.

He went to live with Theo in the latter's modest flat in the rue Laval, to-day the rue Victor-Massé. As there could be no question of his installing a studio there and he was anxious to resume work, he attended, at his brother's suggestion, classes under Fernand Courmon. But he disliked them as much as he had those of the Antwerp Academy, though he made friends with some of his fellow-pupils, such as Anquetin, Toulouse-Lautrec and Emile Bernard. With the latter, eighteen at that time, he later maintained a regular correspondence. Theo also introduced him to independent

LE PONT DE L'ANGLOIS. MARCH 1888. V. W. VAN GOGH COLLECTION, LAREN

LE PONT DE L'ANGLOIS. MAY 1888. WALLRAF-RICHARTZ MUSEUM, COLOGNE

painters. He met Gauguin, Degas, Pissarro and Signac in the shop of the elderly, good-natured Tanguy, who sold artists' materials and befriended his customers. Later on Vincent made the acquaintance of Seurat in a Montmartre restaurant where some of his own canvases were hung. At last he was able to study the impressionist painting Theo had so often mentioned to him. It was still being ridiculed by the public at large and the Parisian critics. But some people were ardently in favour of it. Vincent was lucky to be in Paris that year, which was so important in the history of the movement. For in May 1886 the eighth exhibition of the group, the last before its dissolution, took place. But the disagreements and impassioned arguments, the shocks of personalities and theories, that excited the intellectual and artistic circles of the capital, left the

Mon cher Bernard, ayant promis de
l'écrire, je veux commencer par te
dire que le pays me paraît aussi
beau que le Japon pour la limpidité
de l'atmosphère et les effets de couleur
gais. Les eaux font des tâches d'un
bel émeraude et d'un riche bleu dans les
paysages ainsi que nous le voyons
dans les crépons. Des couchers de soleil
orangé pâle faisant paraître bleu les
terrains. Des soleils jaunes splendides
Cependant je n'ai encore guère vu le
pays dans sa splendeur habituelle d'été
Le costume des femmes est joli et le dimanche
surtout on voit sur le boulevard des
arrangements de couleur très naïfs et
bien trouvés. Et cela aussi sans doute
s'égayera encore en été

Je regrette que la vie ici n'est pas
à si bon marché que je l'avais espéré
et je n'ai pas trouvé moyen jusqu'à
présent de m'en tirer à aussi bon
compte qu'on pourrait le faire à Pont-Aven
J'ai commencé par payer 5 fr et maintenant
je suis à 4 francs par jour. Il faudrait
savoir le patois d'ici et savoir manger de
la bouillabaisse et de l'aïoli alors on
trouverait sûrement une pension bourgeoise
peu coûteuse . Puis si on était à plusieurs
on obtiendrait, je suis porté à le croire, des
conditions plus avantageuses.- Il y aurait
peut être un réel avantage pour bien des
artistes amoureux de soleil et de couleur
d'émigrer dans le midi.. Si les Japonais
ne sont pas en progrès dans leur pays
il est indubitable que leur art se continue
en France . En tête de cette lettre je
t'envoie un petit croquis d'une étude
qui me préoccupe pour en faire quelque
chose . Des matelots qui remontent avec
leurs amoureuses vers la ville qui profile
l'étrange silhouette de son pont levis sur
un énorme soleil jaune
J'ai une autre étude du même
pont levis. avec un groupe de
laveuses . Je serai content d'un
mot de toi. pour savoir ce que
tu fais et où tu iras - Poignée
de main bien cordiale à
toi même et aux amis   bien à toi
                          Vincent

Dutchman cold. He was only interested in the works of Monet, Pissarro, Sisley and Guillaumin, which fairly dazzled him. Their bright and singing colours, the light created by the separation of their brush-strokes, the suppression of local colour, contour and chiaroscuro, the fervour and love of nature evident in the pursuit of its most fugitive effects, were thrilling novelties for Vincent. They were bound to fascinate him. He was also delighted, as a devotee of Japanese art, to find obvious traces of Oriental influence in Parisian painting. He had brought with him the prints on silk bought at Antwerp. He now purchased others to pin on the walls

LE PONT DE L'ANGLOIS. WATER-COLOUR. MARCH–APRIL 1888.
PRIVATE COLLECTION, BERLIN.

LE PONT DE L'ANGLOIS. APRIL 1888. WILDESTEIN GALLERY, NEW YORK
'*As for work, I brought back a 24" × 12" canvas to-day. It's a drawbridge with
a small cart crossing it, against a blue sky. The stream's also blue, the banks
orange and green, with a group of washerwomen in blouses and gaily striped
headdresses.*'
                                                                    Letter to Theo

of his room. Sometimes they appear in the backgrounds of his
portraits. He actually copied three prints, by Hiroshige and Kesai
Yeisen. In painting his own features he deliberately exaggerated
the cheek-bones and the length of the eyes (Cat. 69-76).

At home, in the strict, conventional society of Holland, he had felt stifled. But in Paris, with its ferment of ideas, easy-going habits and extreme freedom of speech, he could breathe. Now that he was relieved of material anxieties, decently dressed, better fed and consequently in better health, as well as being stimulated by the example of others, he was irresistibly impelled to paint and draw. In June 1886 the two brothers moved into a larger flat which Theo had rented at 54 rue Lepic. Vincent turned one of its four rooms into a studio. He had by then ceased to attend Courmon's classes and had all his time to himself. Needless to say, he did not lose a moment of it. From his window he could see the old grey houses that climb the rise of the Butte (Cat. 66). He had only to go out to find the gardens with their box-seats, the lightly railed open ground, windmills with gaily revolving sails, flights of steps and lanes where lampposts stood and the patches of greenery and yellow sand set here and there about the hill. They all provided him with subjects and can be identified in his drawings and paintings. He made ten versions of the famous Moulin de la Galette (p. 45) with the dilapidated wine-shop in opaque red below it (Cat. 53). He found inspiration also along the Boulevard de Clichy

LE PONT DE L'ANGLOIS. MARCH 1888.

LE PONT DE L'ANGLOIS. MARCH 1888.

(Cat. 65), the banks of the Seine, at Asnières (Cat. 85, 86), Suresnes and Chatou (Cat. 85), among factories (Cat. 89, 90) and the wayside inns of outer suburbs (Cat. 82), as well as in the woods and fields of the Ile de France (Cat. 77, 80, 81).

He also composed numerous still-life paintings, which might just as well be self-portraits. For he did not intend to reproduce precisely what he saw. It was always himself that he identified in the model. Bottle and glasses, fish and fruit, tell us both of his frugal habits and the improved quality of his meals. From a *Still Life with Bread, Cheese and Wine,* for instance, we learn that he was now drinking red wine instead of water. In another, *Absinthe* (Cat. 63), we see that he no longer rejected alcohol. He neither concealed nor invented anything. He echoed reality as faithfully as it echoed himself. His work reflects his life, making a public confession of it from beginning to end. Each object he represents mirrors his thought, his feelings, his character and his conduct. In this respect a painting like the *Boots* is significant (see p. 36). Old, worn, gaping and down at heel, the articles exhibited tell a story of

87

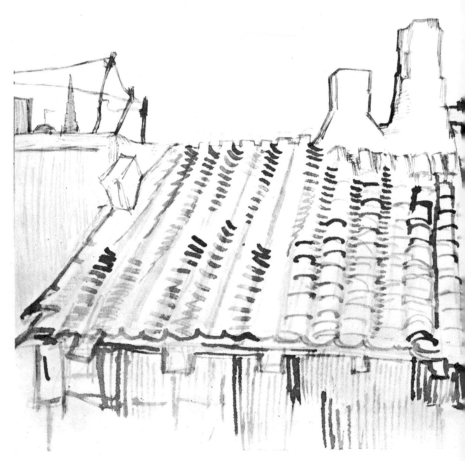

ROOFS. MARCH-APRIL 1888. MR. AND MRS. JOHN REWALD COLLECTION, NEW YORK

poverty, wretchedness and weary, endless tramping. They reveal the plight of the man who wore them out so utterly and, through his adversity, the toil and fatigue of the whole world. In the humblest and most familiar of his models, persons or things, he noted secret affinities with his own being, found himself in them and used them to communicate to others what he felt. When he drew miners, labourers or weavers, he was expressing industrial slavery. When he painted potatoes, he believed himself to be in instinctive contact with the sustaining power hidden in the dark depths of Mother Earth. Till then he had lived in a dim, melancholy and restricted world. Now he was about to step beyond the circle of shadow, led by an unknown painter whose genius he was the first to discover.

In the year of Monticelli's death Vincent had the opportunity to see works by the artist from Marseilles at the Delarbeyrette Gallery in the rue de Provence. On entering the gallery he had the sensation of confronting a different world, some garden of fairyland. He was enchanted by all the splendour he saw, the result of unfailing technical resource, in landscapes shimmering with heat and amazing blossoms for which lyrical ardour rather than botanical knowledge was responsible. They were soon to inspire the Dutch painter. No less than fifty flower-pieces are to be found among his two hundred Paris pictures (Cat. 55-9). A comparison of Vincent's *Flowers in a Blue Vase*, for instance, with the identically named masterpiece by Monticelli shows striking resemblances between them. The vigorous cross-hatching and impasto, the striated, spiral or squirming movements of the brush, the tangled arabesques and the firm draughtsmanship upon which the multiple irradiation of the colours is based are alike in both. After these strenuous stylistic exercises he returned to a more summary, delicate and cursory manner, as in the *Montmartre Fête* (p. 57) and *Montmartre Gardens in Winter* (p. 73), which combine the vivacity of Oriental calligraphy with the subtle chromatic gradations of French impressionism. He had done with leaden backgrounds, thick outlines and crude distortions. He had cleared his palette of the bituminous-black and bistre-brown earth-colours. He had discarded the worn-out black crape mask. Now his observation

ORCHARD IN PROVENCE. APRIL 1888. V. W. VAN GOGH COLLECTION, LAREN

was rapid, his drawing nimble and his colours fresh and softly glowing.

The change had been great during this brief period. So soon after painting the *Boots* he had definitely renounced his dark manner. The morose mood, it seemed, had been dissipated in the new air he breathed. Paris and its intellectual atmosphere, combined with his brother's permanent presence, had done him good. Everything stimulated his energy and curiosity, impelling him to draw and paint, especially to paint. Exhibitions, meetings with the pioneers of modern art, impressionist manifestoes, all the phenomena of this privileged world sharpened his creative faculties. In his endless discussions with Theo he no longer defended local colour, chiaroscuro, humanist realism and the imitation of nature, including, of course, the peasant models he had formerly adored. The flood of new sensations had swept all that away. In his latest revision of opinions he had been influenced by the last comprehensive impressionist exhibition, Seurat's *La Grande Jatte*, his own work with Signac and his confidential talks with Guillaumin. He had listened to Pissarro and watched him put his theory into practice. In the gallery owned by Boussod and Valadon, which Theo managed, he had been able to study at his leisure the chief works of the climax of impressionism.

Vincent must have been greatly attracted by the collective character of that movement, having himself so passionately yearned to belong to a group and work with others. His disappointment must have been equally great when the movement split up. The man hitherto despised, condemned and rejected by his commercially minded countrymen and the paltry conceit of the Dutch artists was in Paris treated as an equal by his colleagues and welcomed with benevolence by the masters of the day. He must have been deeply touched by the generosity of old Tanguy, who supplied him with canvases and colours in exchange for pictures which no one would buy. This excellent man was the first to forsee Vincent's future greatness, putting him on a level, it appears, with Cézanne. It was no wonder that the newcomer could not resist the many spells cast upon him. He made use of such techniques as juxtaposed contrast, complementary colour organisation, divisionism and even the pointilliste methods of Seurat and Signac, defended by Félix Fénéon in a resounding manifesto which Vincent certainly read. These processes appear, particularly, in the *Restaurant Interior* (Cat. 79), the *Basket of Apples* (Cat. 95) and the portraits *Woman at a Cradle* (Cat. 78) and *Tanguy* (Cat. 92). Twenty-two self-portraits record the various influences he underwent during his stay in the French capital. We need only consider the three *Portraits of the Artist in a Grey Hat,* all executed in 1887, to obtain a clear idea of the changes in his style. The impressionist tendency grows more and more distinct as the series proceeds. Even from the expressionist point of view there is a great difference between the attractive, almost elegant personage represented in the first picture (p. 65) and the wild-looking creature depicted in the other two (Cat. 73, 75). The superb *Self-portrait at the Easel* of 1888 simultane-

PROVENCAL ORCHARD. APRIL 1888. V. W. VAN GOGH COLLECTION, LAREN

ously summarises and ends his whole development at that time (Cat. 97). It was a period of research, initiative and elaboration in which the peremptory genius of the artist forced him to an independent position among the novelties of theory and practice he then encountered.

Though he may appear to have joined the impressionists at that time, he did not subscribe to their views in detail. For he soon detected the limitations of a style in which drawing, form and construction were excessively subordinated to the depiction of light and individuality tended to be lost in exclusive devotion to nature. The decisions he took were also influenced, moreover, by his relations with Gauguin. The latter had already declared, with arrogant and convincing assurance, that 'we must leave impressionism behind'. Vincent seems to have looked to impressionism mainly for a corrective to his former errors. It was for the same reason that he studied Delacroix at the Louvre, deliberately imitated Monticelli and borrowed Jongkind's direct and impatient style of brushwork. (See especially the *Moulin de la Galette*, p. 45.) Again, in the *Woman at Le Tambourin* of 1888 the subject recalls Toulouse-Lautrec, while the supple precision of line and the subtle execution would not be unworthy of Degas (Cat. 93). Vincent's powers of assimilation are eloquently displayed in this skilful and elegant picture, painted only three years after the *Potato Eaters*. The *Woman at Le Tambourin* would be less astonishing if it had been signed by a good French painter of the period, some follower of Degas, such as Mary Cassatt, Forain, Rouart or Rafaelli. Yet it may be doubted whether any of them would have succeeded so well.

Paris taught Vincent the optical laws of colour, economy of line and clarity and propriety of expression. It was there, too, that he learned to enjoy painting, to develop the principles of his style and to refine the implements he used. In Paris he also came to know Oriental art better. Japanese culture was then fashionable. The Bing Gallery in the rue de Provence had a permanent exhibition of Japanese prints which Vincent could admire at his leisure. He never tired of examining the dry purity of line, the bright, flat areas of colour and the extreme restraint in execution of these

THE TILE WORKS. APRIL 1888. COURTAULD INSTITUTE, LONDON

works, which completely contradicted the impressionist style. They obsessed him to such an extent that he reproduced some of them in the background to his *Portrait of Tanguy* (Cat. 92) and copied, early in 1888, prints by Hiroshige and Kesai which he had picked up for a few coppers at a second-hand dealer's, as we have already mentioned (Cat. 94, 96). He understood the lessons of the masters of the Ukiyo-e school as well as he did those of Delacroix, Monticelli, Pissarro and Seurat. He adorned the walls of his studio with his beloved Japanese prints on silk and hung them up in a tavern frequented by artists, Le Tambourin. Its manageress, Agostina Segatori, a dark and ardent Italian, became his mistress (Cat. 91). Graduates of the Beaux Arts and earnest disciples of the masters are less apt than the self-taught to profit by the diverse,

95

not to say contradictory, revelations of chance. Vincent was in such an impressionable state while in Paris that he was strengthened and enriched by all the contacts he made. He felt himself to be free of prejudice, receptive to novelty and ready to take any step, however unpredictable. In the more adventurous of his enterprises he sometimes outstripped his age. Thus there is evidence of 'fauvism', before Fauvism was ever heard of, in certain of his canvases, such as *Bastille Day* (*14 July*) *in Paris* (Cat. 88) and *Factories at Clichy* (Cat. 89).

Lastly, it was in Paris that he was able to show his pictures in public for the first time. They were exhibited in the vestibule of the Théâtre Libre founded by Antoine, at Le Tambourin and in a popular restaurant on the Boulevard de Clichy. But they found no more buyers than they had in Tanguy's shop. Neither Vincent nor his colleagues Anquetin, Emile Bernard and Gauguin sold any of their works. But Vincent was especially anxious to do so, though neither out of vanity nor any kind of calculation of his own interest. He could never forget that he was living at Theo's expense. The fact humiliated him and he began to lose heart. Overwork, too, helped to make him nervous and irritable. He was also feeling terribly tired.

What more could Paris now offer him? He was familiar by this time with all its treasures and its glory. He had shared the most intoxicating experiences of those extraordinarily prolific closing years of the century in Paris. As their aftermath sobered him, his powerful individuality rose in revolt. He heard an inner voice warning him that the art of the future could never arise from such disorder and bustle, such masked or distorted faces as he saw around him. An artist, he felt, could only fulfil his task of discovering the truths of creation in his own heart by resorting to the tranquillity of nature and the friendship of his fellow-beings. In cities he found nothing but futility, egotism and the more or less violent conflicts of ambition and self-interest. Vincent could no longer stand the mutual rivalries of his colleagues and the internal quarrels among the impressionists. 'Whichever way you look', he wrote to Emile Bernard in July 1888, 'people are flying at each others' throats with a zeal worthy of a better aim.' With his per-

STILL LIFE WITH LEMONS. MAY 1888. KRÖLLER-MÜLLER RIJKSMUSEUM, OTTERLO.

petual dream of a community of his own, he was naturally distressed by what he called 'these disastrous civil wars'. He adds that the pictures of the future 'will probably be created by groups devoted to carrying out a common plan'. It is natural for a dedicated being to feel solitude most keenly in the crowds of a great city. Consequently, it is not surprising to find Vincent returning to his former preoccupation.

We may ask why so obstinate an individualist, so intent upon developing his own personality and cultivating his basic capacities to their highest potential, should wish to sink his individuality in a group. The question indicates the nature of Vincent's tragedy. Brought up as he was in a Protestant parsonage, he considered he had a right to personal integrity and freedom, yet suffered from conscientious scruples in making any such claim. As an individual he meant to fulfil his appropriate destiny. But as a Christian he condemned his insistence on this aim. The consciousness of sinful pride led to anguish and thence to self-reproach and the desire for atonement. He sought for some means of subduing his own independence and reducing the fortress of egoism in his mind. In other words he, the sinner, would have to be his own redeemer by making an effort towards unification, continuity and coalition with his fellow-beings, by giving them himself and his love. His experiments in love with individuals had failed lamentably. He had attempted in vain to approach God and serve his countrymen. He had only one resource left, that of art. Was not that the most effective way of giving oneself to others, communicating with them and lavishing upon them the profusion of treasure created by talent or genius? And if such gifts were refused, the outstretched hand of a brother ignored, the proffered work received with indifference, the artist should at least share with his own kind the terrible responsibilities he had assumed, so that together they might run the same risks and keep doubt and despair at bay by their common efforts and the reciprocal exchange of feelings and ideas. Such was Vincent's Utopia. But it was nothing more. He himself was fated to betray it by his inconsistencies. René Huyghe quite rightly observed that Vincent was an individual tormented by individualism and yet at the same time exploiting all its resources to their fullest extent. He needed the society he rejected as an individual. He could live neither with nor without it. He can hardly be described except by reference to what cut him off from others. The truth about him resides in his very self-contradiction.

Strangely enough, Theo's company, which had at first soothed him, soon began to irritate him. In a few weeks the brothers were at loggerheads. Vincent was too sincere, uncompromising in his opinions, downright in his remarks, and incapable of accepting current conventions, even as represented by the man he cared for most, to acquiesce in the trivial pretences and concessions of every

FARMHOUSE AND CORNFIELD. MAY 1888. V. W. VAN GOGH COLLECTION, LAREN

day. Theo, on his side, used to a tranquil and orderly life, dreaded disturbance, even that promoted by genius. 'I find this way of living almost impossible', he confided to one of his sisters. As the months passed Vincent grew daily more irascible and more extravagant in his behaviour and conversation. He could not settle down anywhere. He worked less often in the rue Lepic flat, preferring the basement or the quarters of a friend, De Antonio, whom he had met in Courmon's studio and who lived on the top of the Montmartre hill in the Place Saint-Pierre. The brothers frequently quarrelled in the evenings. Vincent may have accused Theo of a lack of faith in his elder brother's work or of conviction in defending it against the criticisms of potential purchasers. But it is doubtful whether Theo could have defended it at all if contemporary evidence is to be believed. Theodore Duret writes in this connection: 'Theodore van Gogh was doing well on the Boulevard Montmartre. But at that time his customers would never have agreed to buy or even take as a gift any of the "horrors", as they called them, which his brother produced. Theo was in any case forbidden by his employers, the Goupils, to stock Vincent's works, which they considered impudent monstrosities, on any of their premises. At the Montmartre gallery Theo could only show them surreptitiously, to close friends. Others he could only store in his flat or send them, on the off-chance of a sale, to Tanguy.'

Such is the explanation of the regard Vincent had for that remarkable personage, whose portrait he accordingly painted on two occasions (Cat. 64, 92), in different styles. He was really more interested in the man himself than in his position as a dealer. Tanguy was a man of humble origin who had supported the *Commune*, the Parisian popular rising of 1871. Disappointed with politics, he had transferred his anticipations of the future to modern art, specimens of which he offered for sale. By nature generous and good-humoured, he had more discernment, despite his lack of education, than the famous critics and collectors of the day. It was he who had introduced Vincent to Emile Bernard and other painters who later acquired renown. Vincent, always a great reader, also improved in Paris his acquaintance with the great French authors, in particular Huysmans and Zola, who each made a deep impression on him. Emile Bernard gives the reason: 'He was attracted in the one by his vigour of style and in the other by his slashing, bitterly satirical, belabouring of really existent types of character; for he always loathed shams. Oddly enough, he cared little for works on a high spiritual level and had nothing to say of the younger poets or even of Baudelaire. At most he accorded them a smile. I understood his attitude better at a later date when he wrote in a letter to me, that art must always be wholesome.'

It seems to have been Vincent's longing for the wholesome and his loathing of shams which made it hard for him to endure Paris. In any case, by the winter of 1887 he had begun to despair. In his fur cap and goatskin cloak he tramped the snow-covered streets in deep depression. He had no idea where to go, where to find a trace of warm human feeling. He had no friends to call upon. His

SUMMER EVENING NEAR ARLES. KUNSTMUSEUM, WINTERTHUR

'Here's another landscape, sunset or moonrise, but summer sun anyhow. Violet town, yellow star, bluish-green sky. All the cornfields have tones of old gold copper, gold-green or red, golden-yellow, bronze-yellow, greenish-red. A No. 30 square canvas. I painted it in a strong mistral with my easel plugged into the ground with iron pegs, a tip I can recommend. You push the feet of the easel into the ground with iron pegs 20 inches long beside them. Tie the whole thing up with string. Then you can work in the wind.' Letter to E. Bernard

colleagues might be as poor as himself, but they had at least some woman or child to care for and the sight of their domestic happiness would be too painful for him. Anyhow, their paltry rivalries disgusted him. As for Agostina Segatori 'she is neither free nor mistress in her own house'. Theo, enslaved by his middle-class prejudices, was 'on the other side of the barricade'. The younger brother was in any case thinking of marrying. Vincent encouraged

VIEW OF ARLES. MAY 1888. SCHOOL OF DESIGN, PROVIDENCE, RHODE ISLAND

the idea. But he seems to have dreaded it as likely to make the weight of his loneliness even heavier.

All the same, Theo's matrimonial project was one of the reasons for Vincent's departure. To take his leave would be the most tactful way of restoring freedom of action to his brother. Apart from this consideration, the time had come for him to try his fortune elsewhere and feed his new passion for colour in a more favourable climate. He was alone and rootless, with no companion or confidential partner but his art. To painting, therefore, he would dedicate his abilities, sacrificing his happiness, his very life, to it. Forsaken as he felt himself to be at this time, he never dreamed for a moment of returning to his native land and his aged mother.

Toulouse-Lautrec had talked to Vincent of the Midi. Well, he would go to the south of France, then. He would find the sun there, a touch of the East, 'the equivalent of Japan'. He wrote: 'I want to see a different light, in the belief that a less clouded sky may enable us to obtain a more accurate notion of the Japanese type of feeling and drawing. In a word, I want to see stronger sunlight.' The air of the Ile de France was too volatile and its light too gentle, so that colours were diluted. Emile Bernard noted later: 'It was the sun, not its beams, that he wished to paint.' Even if he found that hope illusory for the time being he saw no reason why it should not be fulfilled by the foundation of an enterprising colony of artists under the inspiration of Monticelli and with the guidance of Gauguin. The old obsession still dominated him. He clung to it with all the energy of instinctive self-preservation. He was already dreaming of that 'Midi Studio' to which he was later to refer so often. He meant to stake his life on that great undertaking. He ignored the murmured warnings of his reason. He deliberately assumed a blind faith in his ideal, telling himself that nothing would be impossible to men who shared the same passionate belief. Accordingly, he left Paris one cold and dismal February morning, without a ray of sunshine about him or within his heart. He had only two and a half more years to live.

WHEN he reached Arles on the 21st February 1888, Provence was under snow, 'like a Japanese winter landscape'. He at once painted such a picture, one of the first, unquestionably, that he did at Arles (p. 77). Then a gust of the *mistral* brought the sudden southern spring. The Dutchman was dazzled by its magnificence, with the orchards in bloom, the great plane trees bursting with sap, the red earth, like flesh, patched with green and the sky 'a hard blue in the glitter of a splendid sun'. The bright vivacity of re-newed vigour everywhere astonished the man from the north. 'It has something tender and gay about it', he wrote to Theo, adding some lines later: 'It's all new to me. I'm learning and my body's responding gratefully to relatively decent treatment.' He had been abruptly transported to another world. Unshadowed light, clear outlines, brilliant colour, combinations of the greatest possible

VIEW OF ARLES WITH IRISES. MAY
1888. V. W. VAN GOGH COLLECTION,
LAREN

*'Of the town only a few red roofs and a
tower are visible, the rest being hidden
by green fig-trees, all in the background
with a narrow strip of blue sky above.
The town is surrounded by huge meadows
covered by a yellow sea of innumerable
buttercups. In the foreground the meadows are cut by a ditch filled with violet
irises. The grass was being cut while I
was painting, so this is only a study,
not a completed picture such as I meant
to make. But what a subject, eh? The
yellow sea crossed by that line of violet
irises and in the background the quaint
little town with its pretty women!'*
Letter to E. Bernard

harmony and intensity, he had dreamed of it all, known a foretaste of it in Japanese art and now found it in nature itself. All his previous experiences, the 'dark style', 'peasant painting,' the sombre realism of the Dutch school and even the bright realism of the impressionists he had been practising up to a few weeks before, were suddenly swept away. No such rapid and decided a change of inspiration and handling has ever been noted in any other artist. In the first works executed at Arles nothing whatever can be traced of his previous preoccupations.

He had in fact begun to work, the moment he arrived, with 'the lucid and exclusive concentration of a lover'. Going out into the country to paint or draw with a reed, he had found on one of his first excursions a certain drawbridge called locally the *Pont de l'Anglois*. It was an old rustic bridge with walls connected by a wooden platform resting on eight supports and slung by chains from four uprights. The structure, outlined against an azure sky, together with its natural environment, was bound to attract Vincent's invariably alert attention. He made one drawing of it with the reed, another in pencil, a water-colour and five oil paintings. He also sketched the subject in one of his letters to Emile Bernard (see pp. 80-85). The first drawing shows a road bordered with stones along which two figures are walking. In the second drawing the bridge is seen from the opposite side. The painting in the Wallraf-Richartz Museum at Cologne is probably based on this design. A woman is following a cart across the bridge. Green and yellow grass grows on the right bank of the stream. On the left bank two tall, dark green poplars rise. The colours are laid on in broad areas with a full brush. Another version, belonging to V. W. van Gogh, of which there is a copy in a Paris collection, is, however, thinly painted in restrained, smooth, extremely fresh tints, giving an effect of great transparency. The olive-grey masonry to the left carries three figures in dark brown, engaged in conversation. The road is separated from the towing-path by a wide grass verge. A boat in Prussian blue is moored to the right bank. The red-roofed houses and steeple of Arles are seen in the background. The earth is greyish yellow and the sky warm grey. This study, painted in the Japanese manner, depicts the moment

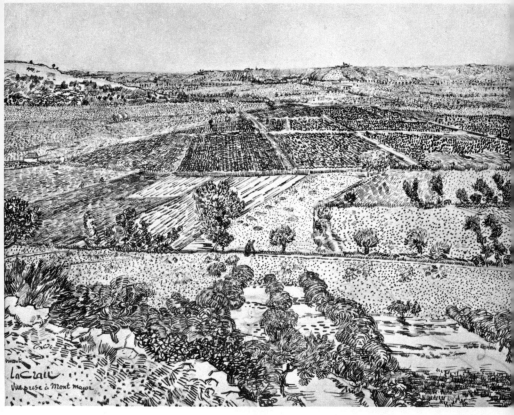

LA CRAU FROM MONTMAJOUR. MAY 1888. V. W. VAN GOGH COLLECTION, LAREN

*'These are views, from a rocky hill, of the Crau, which produces an excellent
wine, the town of Arles and the Fontvieilles country. Contrast of wild, romantic
foreground and distant perspective, wide and peaceful, in horizontal lines falling
gradually to the foot of the Alps.*

*'I believe myself that the two views of the Crau and the country extending to the
Rhone are the best pen work I've done. If by any chance Thomas wants them, he
can't have them for less than 100 francs each. It's not everyone who would have
the patience to be eaten up by mosquitoes and fight the maddening perversity of this
endless mistral, to say nothing of spending whole days out of doors with nothing but
a little bread and milk, as it's too far to be always going backwards and forwards
to the town.'* Letter to Theo

at which the first breath of spring touches the lingering chill of
winter. The two other versions of the *Pont de l'Anglois* are highly
successful. One of them is in the Kröller-Müller Rijksmuseum
and the other in the Wildenstein collection. They vary only very

107

LA MOUSMÉ. JULY-AUGUST 1888.
PUSHKIN MUSEUM, MOSCOW

LA MOUSMÉ. JULY 1888. CHESTER DALE COLLECTION,
NATIONAL GALLERY, WASHINGTON.

CORNER OF A GARDEN. MAY-JUNE 1888. V. W. VAN GOGH COLLECTION, LAREN

slightly. The water-colour is simply a copy in a swifter and more summary style of these two works. It is to the latter, or one of them, that Vincent alludes in his letter of the 10th March 1888 to Theo:

'I brought back a No. 15 square canvas to-day. The subject is a drawbridge with a small vehicle crossing it, outlined against a blue sky, the stream being also blue, the banks orange, with some green. There is a group of washerwomen in blouses and brightly coloured headdresses.'

This masterpiece is worth closer study. The brilliant but not yet hot sunlight flashes like the slice of an unripe fruit. Though objects are precisely outlined, the surrounding air is softly clear and mild. The colours sparkle, but not excessively. The components of the landscape are carefully balanced, presenting an image of virginal nature barely aroused from the torpor of winter and conveying an effect of health, abundance and tranquillity. The 'prodigious joy' he experienced in Provence is to be found elsewhere or at other times. The yellow frame of the drawbridge abuts on supports of grey, yellow and lilac-coloured stone, in relief against a cloudless blue sky. A two-wheeled, horse-drawn vehicle crosses the bridge over a canal with steep banks of orange-yellow soil and green grass. To the right five poplars, still leafless, rise perpendicularly to the wall. To the left, at a lower level, eight washerwomen in brightly coloured garments are beating their linen, making concentric waves in the green water. The play of uprights and diagonals in the suspended construction of the bridge, the contrast of the parallels of the masonry with the contours of the banks, the mutually opposed curves of the boat and the disturbed surface of the water, the blades of grass and reeds rendered in the firm, quick strokes, straight and short, henceforward so characteristic of van Gogh, are all evidence of his executive mastery. He has put in everything, including depth, suggested by the horizon seen through the arch of the bridge, volume, as in his direct treatment of masses, and a nimble, flowing, incredibly confident draughtsmanship. The colours, accurately proportioned and distributed, have retained their vivacity, discreet sparkle and pristine freshness nearly seventy years after the death of the artist. We may add to these virtues an animated yet serene rhythm, in which the more rugged cadences are instantly smoothed out, and a coherent, controlled gaiety, by which the painter meant to convey at that time his complete sympathy with the world, its benevolent welcome to him and his profoundly grateful acceptance of its visual beauty. There are no shadows in the picture, nothing modelled or distorted, not even such broken line and colour as he had been employing a few weeks before in Paris. Nor is there any trace of excitement or uncertainty, or the least sign of obsession. Though he showed eccentricity in his later work and could not always stem the violence or suppress the melancholy of his spirit, the *Pont de l'Anglois* contains no perplexing or disquieting elements. In this painting he was most truly himself.

BOATS AT LES SAINTES-MARIES. JUNE 1888. PRIVATE COLLECTION.

BOATS ON THE BEACH. JUNE 1888. V. W. VAN GOGH COLLECTION, LAREN
'The Mediterranean is the colour of mackerel, that is to say, it varies. One can't always say it's blue, because a second later the reflection changes to pink or grey.'
Letter to Theo

The picture conforms with the artistic ideal he defined so often, in so clear and categorical a fashion. 'Art is only to be found in what is healthy,' he had once told Emile Bernard, who has loyally handed on this observation to posterity. When Vincent later expressed his admiration for the main doorway of the cathedral of St. Trophime at Arles, he at once added: 'But it is so cruel, so monstrous, like a Chinese nightmare, that it seems, grand as it is, to come from another world, to which I'm very glad I don't belong, any more than I do to the vainglorious world of the Emperor Nero.' The writer of these very significant lines did not care much for medieval sculpture nor for the traces of Roman art which to-day attract so many tourists to Arles. He was a man of his time, absorbed in it, too deeply rooted in the present, not to say too bold an investigator of the future, to look to the past. He was incapable therefore of realising that its ruins had once been young like himself and had created a new world, just as his own genius was teaching him to do in his turn. Vincent felt more in tune with art of the Orient, as others also did at that period of ferment. Some, like Gauguin, sought principles of rejuvenation in exotic or primitive art. But Vincent preferred to apply to the Japanese, the most clear-headed, serene and wise of masters. It was of them he immediately thought as he surveyed, with ecstatic delight, almond and peach trees in their pageantry of blossom.

The word 'Japan' is always recurring in his letters. A few days after arriving at Arles he wrote to Emile Bernard: 'I'd like to begin by telling you that I think the country as beautiful as Japan in the limpidity of its atmosphere and the brilliance of its colour.' His northern realism, the naturalism inspired by Zola and the impressionist sensuousness so foreign to his temperament, the memory of everything that had formerly attracted him, was lost in the sparkling and reanimating light of the Mediterranean. It showed him the goal of his deepest aspirations, the soaring lines of his ideal art. It would be 'something peaceful and agreeable, realist and yet painted from the heart, something brief, synthetic, simplified and concentrated, full of serenity and pure harmony, consoling as music.' Was it thus that he defined an art of strain and paroxysm, disordered by impulsive lyrical passion, by a kind of baroque caprice

or ungovernable expressionist violence? Such a picture as the *Pont de l'Anglois* unmistakably refutes this view, a risky one, to say no more of it. And the refutation is supported by everything Vincent painted during this year of splendour, 1888.

He was working 'furiously' now, painting orchards in bloom, with their masses of innumerable, delicate, pink and white petals (p. 93). To secure his easel against the high wind he pegged it down. 'Nothing stops me working, I can't resist such beauty.' The open air did him good. He breathed in great draughts of it, feeling a renewed vigour in his racing blood and, for the first time true happiness. He wrote to tell Theo, Emile Bernard, Gauguin and Toulouse-Lautrec how keenly interested he was. In Arles itself everything delighted him, including 'the zouaves, the brothels, the adorable little Arlesian girls going to their first communion, the priest in his surplice looking like a fierce rhinoceros

THE POSTMAN ROULIN. AUGUST 1888. LOS ANGELES MUSEUM

and the absinthe drinkers.' He was painting fast, for the orchards
would not be in bloom very long. The trees in their undulating,
quivering attire, white or rose-coloured, the impalpable gold dust
dancing in the sunbeams and the tiny, flying corolla-fragments

THE POSTMAN ROULIN. AUGUST 1888. MUSEUM OF FINE ARTS, BOSTON

'A Socratic type and no less so for being rather fond of liquor and possessing a high colour scheme. His wife had just given birth and the worthy fellow was beaming with satisfaction. He's as ferocious a republican as old Tanguy. . . . He was too stiff in the pose, so I painted him twice, the second time at one sitting.'
Letter to E. Bernard

that weave the tapestry of spring are represented in all their fairy-like fragility on his canvases (Cat. 103-6), of which he produced some ten, without counting preliminary studies. In his drawings the line has become surer than ever before, enabling him to give the illusions of contour, volume, space and light in a few strokes. He did a whole series of them with a trimmed reed. In May 1888 he began another series with the pen.

In that month he moved from the Pension Carrel in the rue Cavalerie, to which he had first gone, into rooms at No. 2, Place Lamartine, near the station, forming the right wing of a building (Cat. 107) 'painted yellow on the outside, with a whitewashed interior, full of sunlight'. The floor was paved with square red tiles. But he had to furnish at least one of the four rooms to sleep in. He had spent 600 francs in two months and had no money left. In alarm, he wrote to Theo excusing his extravagance. 'So far I've spent more on canvases, colours and so on than on myself.' He intended to repay his brother by producing as much work as possible for sale. 'I must make my pictures bring in as much as I spend and a bit more.' He despatched all his work to Theo, the paintings in boxes and the drawings rolled up in cardboard. After finishing the set of orchard pictures he collapsed in exhaustion. His digestion had been ruined by wretched food, though he had stopped drinking and was smoking less. As he was penniless, he ceased for the time being to paint and concentrated on drawing.

But he could not resist the innumerable temptations of this wonderful environment, where nature, human beings, the type of clothing worn and all sorts of trifles provided him with subjects 'ready made'. Their colours, the greens and vermilions, above all the yellows and blues, were displayed in seductive profusion on every side. As he gazed upon them he felt an irrepressible desire to assuage his longing to possesses the world by capturing the life that was in them. 'The painter of the future', he exclaims on the 5th May, 'will be such a colourist as was never known before.' He dashed back to work in a frenzy, painting a farmhouse among cornfields and a meadow decked with wild flowers, then the *View of Arles with Irises*, an astonishingly impressive picture which already combines every type of handling and stylistic feature

THE POSTMAN ROULIN. AUGUST 1888.
DR. HANS R. HAHNLOSER, WINTERTHUR

associated with the artist (p. 105). He also painted a number of still-life pictures, possibly his best. They include *Still Life with Coffee-pot, Still Life with a Majolica Pot* (Cat. 108) and the *Still Life with Lemons* (p. 97), which looks so simple and yet is so carefully worked out, with its elaborate scale of yellows enhanced by the dark green bottle and pale green background.

The sun of Provence is already warm in May. The flow of sap to the extremities of every growing plant could be felt by van

THE SEA
AT LES SAINTES-MARIES.
JUNE 1888.
MUSÉES ROYAUX
DES BEAUX-ARTS,
BRUSSELS

HOVELS AT LES SAINTES-MARIES. JUNE 1888. V. W. VAN GOGH COLLECTION, LAREN

Gogh in his own veins, running through him like a flood. His vigour returned and 'with it the idea of success'. His rising lyrical passion made his letters read like odes, the stanzas sounding a note at times which seems almost prophetic:

'I dare say a four-wheeler is useful to some people, those I don't know. But we shan't be mistaken if we believe in the new art, the artists of the future.

'Good old Corot said, a few days before he died: "I dreamed last night of landscapes with a sky all rose-coloured." Well, those rose-coloured skies came along, didn't they, and yellow and green ones into the bargain, with the impressionist landscape? I mean that there are things one feels are going to happen and then they really do. . . .

'There will be art in the future and it ought to be so beautiful and so young that if we actually give up our own youth to it we can only be the gainers, I assure you, in serenity.'

It was always the future that he now wrote about. In Paris he had

FARMHOUSE AT LES SAINTES-MARIES. JUNE 1888. V. W. VAN GOGH COLLECTION, LAREN

stopped thinking about the past and its art. He lived in the present. But barely three months after arriving in Arles he had already left the present for the future. It was by then the only true world for him, one he had himself created. Yet reality had not ceased to exist for him. His health, at any rate, had never been so good. It was perfect at the beginning of June 1888. He was eating in a different restaurant and felt all the better for it. He was working well and had given instructions for both the interior and exterior of his house to be painted before he moved in. This was the 'yellow house' in which he was later to receive Gauguin and other colleagues and to open the 'Midi Studio', the 'studio of the future' of which he still dreamed. Lastly, Arles and its surroundings renewed their fascinations for him every day. He sent enthusiastic descriptions to his brother of the Montmajour rocks at sunset, the Crau plain with its 'broad, quiet perspectives' and 'these endless green and yellow fields'. He succeeded in capturing these last in a painting of admirably subtle luminosity, serene disposition and almost solemn tranquillity, the *Market-Gardens* (Cat. 117). This landscape, resembling a single vast benediction, seems to have arrested the changeful hours and their drifting, linked episodes for ever. That same week he painted the *Field of Corn* (Cat. 114) in which hotter sunlight is rendered by drier colour and more accentuated contrast. These two paintings and the two drawings of the same subjects (pp. 135, 143) prove in equally happy fashion that he was in full possession of his faculties and talents. The same can be said of the various studies made some days previously at Saintes-Maries-de-la-Mer. They include a view of the village nestling close to its Romanesque church (Cat. 110), some thatched and white-washed Provençal farmhouses (Cat. 112), three seascapes with sailing vessels tossing on foam-crested waves (Cat. 111) and lastly two of beached boats (pp. 112, 113), the best of which is in the V. W. van Gogh collection. Vincent had made a preliminary water-colour sketch for it, dashed off at a sitting, without any pointless elaboration.

This work is known all over the world. But no reproduction can ever convey its purity of feeling, exquisite sobriety and dream-like delicacy of handling. The miraculous blend of western inspiration and Japanese economy of statement cannot be brought out by any mechanical process. For the painting expresses the sweetest of poetry in the simplest of language. The vigorous interplay of straight lines and decorative arabesque constituted by the masts, yards and variegated forms of the boats and that of the yellows, greens, purples and blues colouring the latter contrast with the amber hues of the sand and the grey sea flecked with white. The whole scene is saturated in a fluid, pearly atmosphere, under a sky dappled with pallid gleams that tremble like muslin in a breeze.

In this month of June 1888 Vincent painted *Market-Gardens, Field of Corn, Haystacks* (Cat. 116), *The Washerwomen* (Cat. 120), *The Sower* (Cat. 118) in the Kröller-Müller collection and the *Summer Evening Near Arles*, in which the moon coming up over the horizon into a Prussian blue sky behind the violet-tinted town casts ochre reflections across the field that occupies two-thirds of the canvas (p. 101). After executing this splendid landscape he painted the

SUNFLOWERS. AUGUST 1888. NEUE STAATSGALERIE, MUNICH

'*I'm painting just now with the rapture of a* Marseillais *eating* bouillabaisse, *which won't surprise you when you hear that the subject is big sunflowers. . . . I'm working on them every morning, starting at daybreak, for they fade quickly and I've got to do the whole thing right off.*' Letter to Theo

Lawn and the two *Flower Gardens*, in which radiant sunlight kindles the lustre of topaz, amethyst, lapis lazuli, turquoise and fugitive gleams of diamond and sapphire. All the works produced at this time bear witness to the keen vision, controlled passion and consummate skill of the artist. His insatiable appetite for sunshine kept pace with the growing heat of the season. The furnace purified his spirit without consuming it. For the sun of Provence does not parch, enfeeble or destroy. It is the source of energy and rebirth, a fertilising and creative star. Renan said of it that it was the only 'reasonable' image of the divine. Thus Vincent, to give outward expression to his mystic intoxication, invented an *allegro* movement of lines and a triumphal hymn of colours for the most singular sonata in modern painting. 'I even work at midday', he writes, 'in full sunlight, with no shade at all, in the cornfields, and enjoy it all like a cicada.' Then he sighs, thinking of the time he has wasted. 'Heavens, if I had only known this country at 25 instead of 35! But then I used to be crazy about grey, or rather no colour at all. I was always thinking of Millet. And I knew such people in Holland as the painters Mauve, Israels and so forth.' We should be careful not to make any distinction between the draughtsman and the painter in van Gogh. But it was as a colourist that he meant, when he renounced his past, to fulfil his destiny. 'All the colours made fashionable by impressionism', he writes, 'are unstable, which is all the more reason why they should be boldly used raw. Time will mellow them only too well.' It is characteristic of him that his intoxication had not blinded his perspicacity and also that his boldness did not forget precautionary measures. Nevertheless, his pictures were being sharply criticised in Paris. To those who censured his omission of value he retorted: 'It's not possible to have values and be a colourist. One can't be in two places at once.' He added rather spitefully: 'They'll be singing a very different tune one day.'

Ir was natural for his contemporaries to be bewildered and even disgusted by his painting, for he had been the first to work with such indifference to received convention and in so direct a style. He suppressed everything that stood in the way of plain statement

FARMHOUSE IN PROVENCE. 1888. RIJKSMUSEUM, AMSTERDAM

Splendour
~ brilliance

and refulgence of colour, from the moulding of form to chiaroscuro, local colour and half-tone. On the other hand he made use
of every device to free his brushwork and intensify his colours.
He rejected precise description and all embellishment and refinement of subject-matter. He meant only to put down what he felt.
He tolerated no sentimental or intellectual halfway house between
his emotions and the canvas that recorded them. It was the screen
on to which he projected his various moods and the brusque
shocks imparted to his nerves by the spectacle of the world. The
rapidity of his work and its animation even in the slightest sketches
were due to this cause. Yet there is no question of his art being
wholly spontaneous, effusive and undisciplined. Every detail in a
picture breathes with a life of its own, but according to an urgent,
precisely calculated rhythm. The paintings reflect not only his

127

MOORED BOATS. AUGUST 1888. PRIVATE COLLECTION, NEW YORK

physical being but also his mental concentration and deliberation. In his drawing, accessory items being eliminated, every stroke is indispensable to the articulation of form and the expression of the energy accumulated, the tension being such as to suggest vibration long after the initiating impulse. After clearing his palette of muddy tones and insipid gradations of colour, he kept only the purest and crudest of tints, those highest in key, setting them down unadulterated, in abrupt but harmonious contrast, with no attempt at special effects, violence or pointless ostentation. The resultant symphony of reds, indigos, greens, blues and above all yellows differed as much from the classical colour schemes to be found in

MOORED BOATS. AUGUST 1888. FOLKWANG MUSEUM, ESSEN

museums as does the music of orchestral brass from that of a string quartet. The closer the sun came to the earth, concentrating its rays upon the soil of Provence, the more Vincent was inclined to 'overstrain colour'. The glowing countryside, the deep blue sky, the majesty of the glittering, starlit nights, delighted him. 'The future of modern art lies in the Midi,' he exclaimed. He did not regard colour as simply an element of aesthetics, the reflected light of visible objects or the hues they assumed in certain weather conditions or at a given moment. As a realist in quest of that absolute reality beyond the reality of appearance, 'the permanent within the impermanent', he felt that colour had quite a different meaning, possessed a spiritual value, symbolised the essence of being and carried a transcendent message. When he painted orchards in bloom, cornfields, the Montmajour rocks and the Crau plain, sweltering in the heat, swept by the mistral and beset with mosquitoes, he was undertaking a rite such as the ancient sun-worshippers performed in their communion with the principle of light.

He thus came to adore yellow, its colour, that of the fiery disc around which the forces of the universe revolved. It hangs, in his pictures, above the horizon and is repeated in the form of sun-flowers (p. 125). The stars that spangle the night sky in certain of his canvases, as in *The Café Terrace at Night* (Cat. 140) and *Starry Night on the Rhône* (Cat. 142), also resemble so many suns, as do even the ordinary oil-lamps hung from the ceiling in the *All Night Café* (p. 149). In every source of light he saw the heavenly sphere of flame which ripens the harvest, covers the tree with foliage and the earth with flowers, dressing all nature in the rich livery of the seasons and kindling in himself, on his own hearth, a fire of love and impetuous creative force. Nietzsche, another great and lonely man, experienced similar feelings, which he conveyed by verbal imagery. Both the painter-poet and the philosopher-poet resuscitated from a sleep of centuries myths which the ancients had raised to the status of ecstatic representations of the vital impulse. The sun, fire and love are synonymous attributes of divinity. But they are also subjective phenomena. To identify oneself with God, to carry God within one, is to guarantee omnipotence, overcome fear and insecurity, love one's neighbour and have one's love returned. St. Francis of Assisi made the sun itself his brother. In such introspection the individual's past rises from the darkness of memory, bringing with it a whole train of childish recollections. As Vincent confided to Emile Bernard, 'Gusts of remembrance from former days and my aspirations to the infinite symbolised by the sower and the sheaf still fascinate me as much as ever. But when shall I create that picture of a "starry sky" I am always thinking about?' The memories are those of his childhood and the environment into which he was born and received his early education. They are therefore accompanied by a religious turn of phrase.

THE BANK OF THE RHÔNE. 1888. BOYMANS MUSEUM, ROTTERDAM

Emile Bernard observes: 'The letters he wrote to me from Arles often resembled Christian dissertations explicitly reinforcing the idea of religion by that of naturalism in painting. He told me that "Christ worked with a living shape". For him that would be something like painting with a full brush, which he discusses in the same letter in relation to Rembrandt and Franz-Hals. He had returned to the Bible and was extracting symbols from it, being particularly struck by those which referred to the spirit, such as the fish among others, which he was always drawing on the walls of his house. Yellow, the colour expressive of divine brightness, also greatly excited him. "I have had my little house painted yellow", he wrote, "because I want it to be the house of light for everybody." Vincent had been led to such "illuminations" by the silent life he was more or less forced to adopt. For there can be no doubt that the Midi characters he met between Arles and Tarascon were very far from congenial to, in fact just the reverse of, the spirituality of his northern temperament.'

The southerners who slighted him, understood him so little and responded so indifferently, so ill-naturedly sometimes, to his advances were nevertheless regarded by him with deeply sympathetic curiosity. He spoke of them with affectionate indulgence. It was true they knew nothing of art. But 'they are much more artistic in their appearance and way of life than people in the north. I have seen faces here as fine as those in Goya and Velasquez . . . and women like those of Fragonard and Renoir.' He wrote to Emile Bernard: 'At Saintes-Maries there were girls who made me think of Cimabue and Giotto, they were so slender and upstanding, with a touch of sadness and mysticism about them.' What penetrating observation and telling description in a few words! His verbal account of the *Zouave* painted in June 1888 is as good as the portrait. 'A little bull-necked fellow with a tigerish eye.' He goes on to refer to the picture: 'The half-length I painted of him was frightfully harsh. The blue of his uniform was like that of an enamelled saucepan, the gold lace a tarnished orange-red, the two stars on his chest an everyday sort of blue, very difficult to render. I put his feline, deeply tanned head, with its madder cap, against a green door and an orange brick wall. The violent combination of dissonant colours was not easy to manage. The study I made struck me as very harsh. But I would always rather work on such vulgar, even discordant, portraits like this' (Cat. 119). We certainly have here a fresh proof, if one were needed, of Vincent's conscious, deliberate and calculated audacity, though he has been called an artist incapable of controlling his impulses and frenzy. In connection with the *Zouave* painting some further observations come to mind.

At Arles Vincent at first painted landscapes to express the spell cast upon him by rejuvenated nature and his intimate participation in the generative action of the sun. For the same reasons he proceeded to make a number of studies of the *Sower* theme. But he also wished to represent the human types around him. On the 4th May 1888 he wrote to Theo: 'I believe I may be able to paint some portraits here'. In the following month, after working for a week in the cornfields, he sketched the outline of a sower on ploughed land, 'a great field of violet clods of earth . . . on the horizon a

PORTRAIT OF LIEUTENANT MILLIET. SEPTEMBER 1888.
KRÖLLER-MÜLLER RIJKSMUSEUM, OTTERLO

field of ripe corn . . . above it all a yellow sky with a yellow sun'
(Cat. 118). The subject haunted him, going beyond his artistic aim
and stimulating his latent mysticism. He wondered whether he
had better not paint a 'terrible picture' of it. 'Heavens, how I long
to do one!' He laid the foundations for this 'terrible' picture by
making numerous drawings (p. 194) and several painted studies.
'After Millet', he observes, 'one can only do a sower in colour,
juxtaposing yellow and violet, for instance . . . but if so one lands
in a Monticellian metaphysics of colour, a sloppy mess from which
it's devilish hard to emerge with honour.' The phrase 'metaphysics
of colour' will be useful to remember as an aid to further explora-
tion of the mystery of van Gogh. But the figure of the sower,
whether regarded as element of landscape or symbol, is not a
portrait.

The first portrait Vincent painted at Arles was the *Zouave* already
mentioned. In August 1888 he made a second and improved
version. The same soldier, with his dark blue tunic, baggy trousers,
bright red skull-cap and white gaiters, posed on a red-tiled floor
against a white wall (Cat. 121). The work is a masterly one, unusual
for the period. Neither Delacroix nor Manet, not even Cézanne or
Gauguin, would have ventured upon so violent a chromatic
arrangement. Yet its aggressive boldness is full of vigour, sanity
and confidence. We must be careful not to impute systematically
provocative intentions to the artist. He turns, actually, from the
trenchant harshness of the *Zouave* to the *Mousmé* of July 1888, representing a charming little Provençal girl whose portrait he
painted after reading *Madame Chrysanthème*, by Pierre Loti. The
picture is one of extreme delicacy, suavity and elegance. The graceful elongation of the arms and the curvilinear stripes of the bodice
make a harmonious contrast with the freely spiralling lines of the
rattan armchair, while pastel shades are used to bring out the girl's
virginal freshness. The drawing that preceded this painting is even
more fascinating (p. 108). Great as the painter is in this case, the
draughtsman unquestionably surpasses him.

Vincent executed six portraits in all (Cat. 134, 165) of the postman Roulin, an excellent man who became his friend and remained
loyal to him through the worst of his misfortunes. In the most

HARVEST IN PROVENCE. JUNE 1888. PRIVATE COLLECTION

important of these paintings Roulin is represented at three-quarter length 'in a blue uniform with gold ornamentation, coarse features, bearded, very Socratic type' (p. 117). Seated in an arm-chair with his left arm resting on a green table, the sturdy figure outlined against a greyish-blue background and the blue mass of the uniform set off by its bright yellow buttons and stripes, the model appears really attractive in his innocent pride. Vincent painted later portraits of equal solidity and distinction but never one of such superb quality. Roulin's entire family posed for him subsequently, including his wife, his two sons Armand and Camille and the baby, Marcelle (Cat. 154, 155, 156, 160). We may select, further, from the famous series of portraits, that of *Lieutenant Milliet* (p. 133), pale-faced, posed against a thickly

THE POET'S GARDEN.
SEPTEMBER 1888. KRÖLLER-
MÜLLER RIJKSMUSEUM,
OTTERLO

'*The bush is green, with a
bit of bronze and other colours. The grass is very, very
green, Veronese lemon-green,
and the sky is very, very blue.
The row of bushes in the background are all oleanders, mad
as hatters, the damned
plants flower so crazily they
might easily get locomotor
ataxy. They're loaded with
new blossoms, as well as
heaps of faded ones, and the
leaves, too, are being renewed
by vigorous new shoots to
which there appears to be no
end. A funereal, completely
black cypress towers above
them and a few small coloured
figures are strolling along a
pink path. . . .*
'*But don't you think it's an
amusing kind of garden, one
where it's easy to imagine
Renaissance poets like Dante,
Petrarch and Boccaccio strolling between the bushes over
the flower-decked grass?*'
Letter to Theo

painted emerald background, and that of *Eugène Boch* (Cat. 141), a Belgian painter and poet who lived in a village near Arles. His delicately shaped, sharp-featured head is silhouetted against a starry sky of deep ultramarine. The stars indicate Vincent's sympathy with the poet 'who dreams great dreams' as well as with the man for his own sake. 'Instead of painting the commonplace wall of a room behind the head', he explains, 'I painted infinity.' After thus speaking as a poet, he adds as a painter: 'I made an arbitrary choice of colour in the finishing touches, exaggerating the fairness of the hair with orange, chrome and pale lemon.'

A month previously in August 1888, he had already taken the same risk, defying nature in the portrait *Old Provençal Peasant* (Cat. 132). 'Imagine', he writes to Theo, 'this formidable character that I had to paint during the furnace of harvest-time and at midday too. That's why I used those oranges blazing like red-hot iron and the luminous tones of old gold in the dark passages. Well,

SHEAVES OF CORN. 1888. DR. HANS R. HAHNLOSER COLLECTION, WINTERTHUR

HARVEST. JUNE 1888. HENRI MATISSE COLLECTION, NICE

well, my dear brother . . . I suppose nice people will consider my exaggerations simply caricature.' He wonders how the Parisians will take his 'sunburnt' canvas. He expects them to give a start of terror at the ferocity of the rough hatching, the deliberately emphasised distortions and the no less deliberately feverish colour. 'Too bad they never cared much for that rugged stuff like Monticelli's and the splash and mash school . . . pity there's not more "clog" painting in Paris!'

He put on his 'clogs' again to paint *Young Man With Cap* (p. 141) in which the provocative violence of drawing and colouring increases the impact of this painting of an elfin countenance in broad, rapid brush-strokes. In this case it seems as though the artist, in his scorn of the pretence of good taste characteristic of a decadent epoch, took a sly pleasure in coming close to vulgarity. But it would be a mistake to suppose that he did nothing but 'clog' painting or carried his arbitrary invention to the point of disorder and his exaggeration into extravagance. Every one of the portraits painted during this period is entirely coherent, planned and homogeneous in its proportions, forms and colours. In the *Old Peasant*, for example, his hand may seem to run away with him, teasing the texture, so to speak, with a series of 'bristling' touches. But this procedure was a deliberate attempt to convey the flamboyance of his vision. He is just as capable of composing relaxed and tranquil images like the *Mousmé* and the *Girl,* the latter set against a rose background (Cat. 128) (Kröller-Müller Museum).

No artist ever dared to work under such unfavourable conditions. The mornings and evenings were suitable enough for painting, but hardly the midday and nocturnal hours. The spell of Provence did not end, for him, after spring was over. The unbearable heat of summer, so far from discouraging him, appeared to refresh and stimulate him. The glimpse of an outline, a cornfield, a flourishing hedge-row, sun-browned stones, insects fluttering in the grass or even a simple effect of light would send him rushing, in an ecstasy, to canvas or paper. He toiled incessantly, frantically and indefatigably. 'I'm very, very well', he told Theo. But he must have been enduring severe privations. He lived on nothing but ships' biscuits, milk and a few eggs all that August. But so long as he could keep fatigue at bay and 'retain a clear feeling of the stars and infinity above' he did not care. He could always smoke his pipe over a glass at the end of a gruelling day and occasionally seek illusory solace 'with female types at two francs a time'. And then

YOUNG MAN WITH CAP. 1888. COLLECTION OF FRITZ NATHAN, ZURICH

Gauguin, 'my friend Gauguin', was about to rejoin him. Vincent was certain by now that with Gauguin he would be able to found that 'Midi Studio', to be a refuge for poor artists vegetating in Paris. Then at last he would no longer be alone. A heartfelt cry escapes him. 'Life's something like a miracle, after all!'

He had a lot of trouble in finding models. For as soon as the people of Arles saw his pictures, they refused to pose. 'They considered I was making a mess of it by only doing *pictures with nothing but paint in them. . . .*' Even 'decent whores' kept out of his way. But did he lose heart? Not a bit of it. 'I'm going ahead like a painting steam-engine', he writes. In the absence of models he put up his easel in the country, in the public parks (see *The Poet's Garden*, p. 137), in the streets or on the quays on the Rhône. He was never tired of watching the glow of objects in this sunny world, the definition of their shapes, the precision of their contours and the transfiguration of their local colour. All such effects stripped them of falsehood, making them seem new and eternal. The relative and the ephemeral dropped away. The real, in all its integrity, revived. Fields and sheaves of corn turn to blocks of petrified lava in his pictures (Cat. 122, 123). Stacks crystallise the solar rays which have fertilised them and swell out like halos of gold (Cat. 124). An endless glitter fills the air. Nothing is more compact, less fugitive or so fantastic as this restored reality, solidified like clay fired in the kiln.

At the height of summer he produced a study of dusty thistles growing in waste land, with a swarm of white and yellow butterflies about them (Cat. 126) and another of a garden nook bright with flowers, also haunted by butterflies (Cat. 131). He painted *Moored Boats* on the Rhône (p. 129), *Caravans* (Cat. 135), a bunch of oleanders (Cat. 130) and lastly the *Sunflowers* series (p. 125). He explains as follows why he treated this theme so often. 'I'm thinking of decorating my studio with half a dozen paintings of sunflowers in which the pure or broken chrome yellows will sing against different backgrounds of blue, from the palest Veronese to royal blue, framed in orange-coloured wood.' He considers the effect will resemble that of the Gothic rose-window. For in his view the significance of these large flowers goes beyond that of the

CORNFIELD. JUNE 1888. J. W. BÖHLER COLLECTION LUCERNE

ordinary still-life. He worships the sun and its colour, the yellow colour of light, health and incessant renewal. When he exclaims, at the height of his rapture, 'How beautiful yellow is!' he is not only speaking as a painter, but also as a man ecstatically proclaiming his desire to possess the whole of creation, penetrate its essence and assuage therein his 'need of gaiety, happiness, hope and love', as he seeks to transcend his material distress. 'The uglier, the older, the more ill-natured, infirm and poor I become, the more I long to compensate myself by producing resplendent and well arranged colour.' It was then that he achieved the 'high yellow note' he mentions, as though all the fires of heaven had entered him to kindle it. 'How glorious the sun is here at the height of summer! It goes to my head like a blow. I don't wonder people

143

get sunstroke.' He has reached the point of reciprocating nature's own gift of exaltation.

The fever of his senses affected his brain. He realised that life is short and that the sacrifices made by artists are of no avail to them. But 'if only we enable the artists who follow in our footsteps to lead fuller lives we shall have accomplished something.' Still, he had one hope left, that of 'painting in better conditions, in another life.' The sun-worshipper was by now rising to a mystical level. The God of his childhood revived in the depths of his soul, illuminating his thoughts. He reflected that the artist's sufferings on earth are not pointless but designed by destiny. Vincent, a true Christian, never uttered a rancorous word. Referring to himself, Gauguin and other painters, he philosophically observes: 'We

WOMAN READING. NOVEMBER 1888. PRIVATE COLLECTION, PARIS

RED VINEYARD. NOVEMBER 1888. PUSHKIN MUSEUM, MOSCOW

must above all explore our own hearts, our good will and our patience.' Goodwill, patience, and also work, were required. He himself never rested or allowed anything to distract him from his efforts. 'All the same', he confesses, 'I feel a terrible need of—dare I pronounce the word?—religion. At such times I go out of doors at night to paint the stars.'

It was then, in September 1888, that he began his 'starry nights' series notably the *Café-Terrace At Night* (Cat. 140). The premises, formerly in the Place du Forum, have since disappeared. The terrace was lit by 'a big gas-lamp in the blue of night, a corner of starry blue sky visible.' He also painted *Starry Night on the Rhône*

145

LANDSCAPE WITH TELEGRAPH POLES. JUNE 1888. V. W. VAN GOGH COLLECTION, LAREN

(Cat. 142). The amazement of the citizens may be imagined when they saw him setting up his easel at unearthly hours on the pavement, illuminating his canvas with candles fixed in his hat. He said himself that he considered the night 'much more animated and richly coloured than the day' and that the sight of the stars filled him with hope. That September he painted the *All Night Café*, representing unquestionably the Café de l'Alcazar in the Place Lamartine. 'The room is blood-red and dull yellow, with a green billiard-table in the centre and four lemon-yellow lamps casting an orange and green light.' He adds the remarkable observation that 'the colour is not locally true to life in the naturalistic manner but suggests some kind of ardent emotion'. The note applies with even greater propriety to the water-colour he made of the same subject

(p. 149), where space is deeper, forms more simplified and colour less broken, more strikingly contrasted and utterly fresh into the bargain. A month later he painted another interior, but from memory. It represented the reception room of a brothel, with men and women seated at tables drinking (*Le Lupanar*).

Owing to lack of money, he had not yet been able to move in to his house. He was worried over this matter, because Gauguin would soon be coming. It was therefore with intense delight that he received a further remittance from his brother. It would enable him to buy some furniture at last. He lists the items with childish satisfaction, going complacently into the details of decoration, for the 'House of Friends' he had so longed for must welcome its occupants and make them comfortable. He invited Theo forthwith. 'You will find it full of sunlight', he writes, or else 'with lighted window under the stars'. He describes Theo's room. 'Big yellow sunflowers decorate the white walls. When you open the window in the morning you'll see the green of the gardens, the rising sun and the entrance to the town.' In the excitement of realising his dream, he overflows with energy and enthusiasm. 'I'm getting lots of ideas for work.' Such a man could not be unhappy. Even when he looked on the black side of life he saw it through a veil of exultation.

He felt so pleased and sure of himself that he no longer asked for advice, but actually preferred to give it. By now he was not begging for encouragement but distributing it himself, either directly to Emile Bernard or indirectly to Gauguin, preaching constancy, moderation and discretion. To Theo, whose health was again deteriorating, he addressed letters full of reassuring optimism, to the effect that his brother as 'dealer and apostle' and he himself as artist would one day have their reward. 'We must control our impatience meanwhile and be careful how we behave, that's essential for both of us.' Though he does not forget that Theo supports him, he considers the arrangement justified. 'When you give to an artist you are acting as one. All I hope is that my canvases may become such as will render you not too discontented with your own work . . . so you must tell me to stop if I go too far.' Theo replies with equally touching solicitude. Their correspond-

VINCENT'S CHAIR. DECEMBER 1888–JANUARY 1889. TATE GALLERY,
LONDON

'*Meanwhile I can tell you, all the same, that these two last studies are quite
amusing. Both canvases are the same size. One is just a single wooden, straw-covered
chair, yellow all over, standing on red tiles against a wall. Daylight. The other's
Gauguin's armchair in red and green, done at night. Wall and floor also red and
green. Two novels and a candle lying on the chair.*'
Letter to Theo

ALL NIGHT CAFE. WATER-COLOUR. AUGUST-SEPTEMBER 1888.
COLLECTION OF DR. A. HAHNLOSER, WINTERTHUR

'In my picture of an all-night café I've tried to suggest that it's a place where you can be ruined, go mad and commit crimes. In short, by contrasting soft rose and the red of blood and wine-dregs, mellow Louis Quinze and Veronese greens with greenish-yellow and hard blue-greens, in a hellish, sweltering atmosphere of pale saffron, I aimed at something like the powers of darkness in a low drinking-den, lurking under the appearance of Japanese gaiety and Tartarinesque good humour.'
Letter to Theo

ence is like a cantata for two voices answering each other in dulcet harmony, at due intervals in the affectionate dialogue. Theo fears that his brother, in his rapt concentration, may be neglecting the most elementary necessities. 'You must have been working so hard that you forgot to take care of your health', he writes on the 23rd October 1888. 'Your financial plans are wonderful. But what worries me is that for all that you're always on the rocks because you can't stop helping others. I'd like to see you more of an egotist before you get on your feet.'

Each brother was anxious about the other's health, the elder reproaching himself for living at the younger's expense and Theo excusing himself for not doing enough and terrified in case his brother collapsed from overwork in the superhuman effort to deserve his confidence. Vincent knew that without Theo's support both his work and his life would come to an end. Theo knew that his support was paradoxically responsible for an excessive, potentially dangerous strain on his brother's part. For to Vincent only the maximum could be enough. No other artist has in fact produced such a body of work in so short time, in such quantity, variety and consistently high quality. If his career had ended with the summer of 1888, it would have been no less glorious. Yet he was still to execute, during his two remaining years of life, hundreds of pictures and drawings, some of which are indisputable masterpieces.

Six months after coming to Arles he continued to be fascinated by all he saw there. One evening, after he had spent the day painting a new canvas, he wrote in exhilaration: 'Nature here is *extraordinarily* beautiful, all of it, everywhere. The dome of the sky is an admirable blue. The rays of the sun are pale saffron. . . . I'm beginning to feel quite a different person from the man I was when I first came. I have no more doubts and never hesitate when I start anything. . . . I'm so happy with this house and my work. . . .' He goes on to write at length of the pictures he is painting and the studies he is going to make in the public park and gardens. He describes cedars and cypresses of dark green in the brilliantly green grass and the 'crazy' oleanders flowering at the end of the path. 'To-day again', he continues, 'I've worked from 7 in the morning till 6 in the evening, only stopping once to take a bite round the corner . . . at present I see my work with perfect clarity and love it blindly. This coloured environment is quite new for me and I am extraordinarily elated by it. I'm never tired. I'm going to do another painting this very night.' Referring to the portrait of Lieutenant Milliet he was then finishing, he adds: 'How I wish you could see everything I see nowadays! There is so much beauty before me that I can do nothing but pursue it.'

The above quotations may seem to have been unnecessarily prolonged. But they are essential for a proper understanding of

WASHERWOMEN. JUNE 1888. KRÖLLER-MÜLLER RIJKSMUSEUM, OTTERLO

Vincent's life, both internal and external, during this fortunate year of 1888. We must make a clear distinction between what he experienced and what he desired, between his impulse to embrace and retain for ever all the splendours of the world and his decision

RAILWAY BRIDGE
TARASCON ROAD
OCTOBER 1888
ERICH-MARIA REMARQUE
COLLECTION, NEW YORK

THE ZOUAVE. JUNE-JULY 1888.

MR. AND MRS. JUSTIN K. THANNHAUSER COLLECTION, NEW YORK

to pay by his own labour the debt he owed his brother. We must not forget that it was both passion and a sense of duty that drove him to paint. He therefore spent his strength without counting the cost. Painting was a necessity to him. But he also painted in the hope of selling his pictures and thus reimbursing Theo for the latter's beneficence and ensuring a decent life for each of them. He laments that the goal is still far off. But until he reaches it he will have to 'produce and produce much and keep on producing'. He did not mean that production should be over-hasty and indiscriminate. He was only able to work at such prodigious speed because his inspiration and skill allowed him to do so. He never lost control of his instinct for a moment. Before acting he always consulted his conscience. 'I have a frightful lucidity at times', he writes, 'when nature is so beautiful as it is now. Then I lose all awareness of myself. The picture comes to me as in a dream.' But he exercised a prudent and intelligent self-discipline on such occasions, telling himself not to hurry or force anything, to be patient. When he exclaims, 'I've finished ten canvases!' his pride is not in the quantity but in the quality of the work.

After this active period of production he was once more obliged to call a halt. He had used up all his materials and money. For four days he lived only on coffee and a little bread bought on credit. Theo mildly reproved him. He answered: 'If you could see my studies you would tell me I was right to work at white-hot concentration while the fine weather lasted.' It was still fine in the autumn. Vincent contemplated with ardour the strange reddish colour of the earth, the yellowing trees, the dead leaves flying before the mistral and the gold and purple sunsets. 'It's at least as beautiful as the orchards in bloom', he notes with a groan. 'I can't stop all of a sudden.' He drew a garden with two bottle-green cypresses, three orange chestnut-trees and a yew with pale lemon-coloured foliage, then another garden bright with geranium beds. Near his house, which he had painted the previous month (Cat. 136), he proceeded, in October, to paint *The Railway Bridge*. It was an unpromising subject, which he treated in masterly fashion with simplified drawing and sober colours dominated by a key of greyish green, thus calling attention to the opposing perspectives

PORTRAIT OF THE ARTIST WITH STRAW HAT. 1888. V. W. VAN GOGH
COLLECTION, LAREN.

of the Tarascon road and the transverse platform of the bridge (p. 153). The picture is solidly constructed and executed with great ease in a flowing quality of paint. Practically the same style is applied to *Pont de Trinquetaille* (Cat. 149). But he returns to colour in the *Bedroom*, of which he painted a second version a year later at St. Rémy (p. 181). 'The colour is flat and pure, as in silk-paintings,' he said. And in fact here for the first time, perhaps, an interior was painted with shadows and modelling entirely suppressed and perfectly smooth, glowing areas of colour disposed in purely arbitrary fashion. The tones were of course invented by the artist without reference to those he actually saw. In any case there is no sign in this picture of the striated, jerky, hatching brushwork so characteristic of Vincent elsewhere. The tints are all uniform, emphatic, vigorously brushed in with a ductile consistency of the oil medium. He intended by this process to render 'things in a bigger style', thus suggesting repose and sleep. 'The picture', he explains, 'should give the spectator's head, or rather his imagination a rest.' It was an idea, we may note in passing, very close to the theory of painting taught by Matisse. But it will be only those led astray by ill-regulated reading who will be surprised to find van Gogh commending an art of balance and peace, a tranquillising specific for the mind.

It cannot be said that all the works of this period resemble those just mentioned. Nevertheless, even pictures in quite a different style, such as *The Caravans*, *The Tarascon Stage-coaches* and also *The Poet's Garden* (p. 137) make an identical impression of force, logic and sanity. *Les Alyscamps* (Cat. 151) is also comparable, with its summary perspective and two dominant notes of green and orange. So are the series of portraits including *Camille Roulin* (Cat. 154) and *Armand Roulin* (Cat. 156). Van Gogh the 'exasperated painter' and 'first of the Expressionists' cannot be traced in these fine portraits, where there are no indications of violent movement or passionate emotion. There is nothing to be seen but stable, impassive, rigidly designed forms and solidly built up volume. Expression is confined to the pictorial arrangement, the disposition of the figure, the surrounding space, the component proportions, linear direction and speed, tonal registration and relationships.

In the self-portraits, however, a very distinct change occurs. At this period his spirit was at one with nature, his body unflagging in its obedience to his will, his genius readily respondent to the stimulation of a kind of dedicated zeal. We may wonder, therefore, why the spell should be broken and his whole serenity lost as soon as he came to reproduce his own features. On such occasions it it seems that, in spite of his general sense of well-being, a latent melancholy came suddenly, without his realising it, to the surface of his mind. Perhaps the burning desire to overtake life, the feeling that it continually eluded his most desperate efforts to grasp it, were responsible for the tragic accent in these paintings. Those produced at Antwerp, and later in Paris, even *Portrait of the Artist with a Grey Hat* (p. 65), which is nevertheless the least embittered, the most juvenile, of all, give an impression of anxiety and anguish. As for that painted in 1888 at Arles, in which he wears a straw hat, the ferocious, uneven, twitching brush-strokes express a challenging, aggressive savagery (p. 156). An even more

MONTMAJOUR. JULY 1888. PRIVATE COLLECTION, AMSTERDAM

CRAG. JULY 1888. V. W. VAN GOGH COLLECTION, LAREN

significant self-portrait, that dedicated to Gauguin (see frontis-
piece) was executed in September 1888, the very month in which
he painted *The Yellow House, The Tarascon Stage-coaches, The Poet's
Garden* and *Lieutenant Milliet,* all works in which he proclaims his
healthy enjoyment of life in general and of the beauties of Provence
in particular.

Gauguin has sent him a self-portrait and Vincent dedicated one
to him in exchange. It represents him bare-headed and bare-necked,
with slanting eyes and prominent cheek-bones, the cheeks and chin
covered with an irregular growth of shaggy, bristling, reddish hair.
The harsh, emaciated, deeply hollowed features, with their heavily
accentuated planes, 'ashen grey against pale Veronese', were said

159

PORTRAIT OF THE ARTIST WITH SEVERED EAR. JANUARY 1889. COURTAULD
INSTITUTE, LONDON

by Vincent himself to resemble 'those of a bonze, a simple wor-
shipper of the eternal Buddha'. The face might indeed be that of
some wild hermit painted by Liang K'ai or Kuan Yu. Yet Vincent
considered it 'as serious as but less despairing than' Gauguin's.
He writes: 'What I mainly feel in Gauguin's portrait is that he must
not continue to be like that, but must pull himself together and
become once more the more prosperous Gauguin who painted

negresses.' What an optimist he must have been himself to deplore
Gauguin's excessive pessimism! He adds: 'The portrait makes
Gauguin look ill and in pain. But that won't last. It'll be very
interesting to compare this one with the one he'll do of himself
in six months' time.' But what Vincent had said of Gauguin's face
might have been repeated by the latter, with more reason, of van
Gogh's. For the Dutchman's self-portrait is a terrible, if involun-

tary, confession. In spite of the happy conditions in which it was painted the atrocious truth comes to light in the picture, as though destiny itself had tricked the artist by replacing him at the easel.

All the self-portraits of van Gogh in fact tell the same story, that of a man whose sincerity passes belief. His frankness was comprehensive, brutal, terrifying. It revealed the individual stripped bare of all appearances, unvarnished, frightening and obscene in its nudity. Whatever the nature of these paintings and whenever they were executed, the subject always looks haggard and taciturn, the hard skin tightly stretched, the mouth bitter, the ears flattened like those of an enraged cat, the red hair dry as a thatched roof and a strange depth in the grey-blue glance, of a disquieting, mechanical fixity. It is the face of a man who has fought incessantly without winning and yet already come to terms with life. He seems both victorious and vanquished, either rejecting victory or still seeking it. He himself pronounces his obituary. 'He was born under a curse. He lived under it and died of it. There was not the least reason for his existence. He was not wanted in the world. Though his life was superfluous no one ever gave him a chance to emerge from it. Pity him!'

SINCE coming to Arles he had accumulated some two hundred paintings and drawings, an average of one a day. It was a remarkable feat considering the calls upon his time due to his economic difficulties and the periods when he had no money to buy new materials. The quantity of work he did in these conditions was accordingly enormous, even leaving out of account sketches and rough drafts, botched or unfinished canvases and the fact that all his productions bear the unmistakable signs of attentive, scrupulous and confident handling. The explanation of the mystery, of the amazing skill he showed so soon after setting foot in Provence, lies in the eight years of resolutely sustained effort undergone in the studies and exercises which enabled him to refine his vision and learn his technique. He had masters at The Hague and at Antwerp. But he paid no attention to their lessons. His real masters were Monticelli and, above all, the Japanese. He examined the works of the latter at length, accepted their severe discipline and

GARDEN. JULY 1888. OSKAR REINHART COLLECTION, WINTERTHUR

assimilated their traditional artistic principles. It is now known that the Japanese painters invariably preceded composition by intense mental concentration. As soon as they had penetrated the subject-matter deeply enough to comprehend its essence, they started painting without hesitation or fumbling, with nimble, rapid and decided brush-strokes. Vincent again and again expressed his admiration for and envy of their prodigious dexterity and their ideals of simplicity and calm. It was to their example that he owed his disconcerting swiftness of execution, needing no revisions or second thoughts, and his habit of painting the same picture five or six times rather than retouching it.

'I shall have to learn', he wrote, 'to draw a figure in a few lines, and I'm on the track of it.' Whenever he feels he is making progress, he at once notes the fact. 'My attention is becoming closer and my hand surer.' He soon reached the stage of painting *The Postman Roulin* at a single sitting. He announced his feat to Theo, with pride, on the 15th August 1888. He only needed a single morning to start and finish one of his *Sunflowers* series and *Pont de Trinquetaille*. He was aware that he might be blamed for working too fast. 'Don't believe it', he writes to his brother. 'It's emotion, the sincerity of feeling for nature, that guides the hand. If such feelings are some-times so strong that the work goes on unconsciously, the brush-strokes succeeding and related to one another like the words in a speech or a letter, one must remember that it was not always so. . . .' Some days later he writes: 'Don't think I get into a feverish state of mind artificially. It's just that I'm continually absorbed in complicated calculations that produce a rapid succession of rapidly painted pictures which have been thought over for a long time in advance. So when people tell you a picture has been done too quickly, you can answer that they've given it too quick a look.' There is no need to stress the importance of this passage, which clearly reveals the secret of van Gogh's virtuosity, in the best sense of the word. Again and again he exclaims: 'I've only to let myself go . . . the picture comes to me like a dream. 'At the end of the summer of 1888 he utters a cry of triumph. He finds he need no longer draw the design in charcoal on the canvas. He embarks on it 'with the colours themselves'.

Vincent, after thus undergoing a second education by the Japanese, the most adroit of painters, was working, like them, with an ease, rapidity and assurance which had already been acknow-ledged, in their case, by Europe. He never ceases to refer to them and confess what he owed them. As already mentioned, he had copied prints by Kesai Yeisen and Hiroshige. He had borrowed from the Japanese some of their favourite themes, the insect, the crab, the blade of grass and the branch of almond-blossom. He used a reed to give his brushwork the boldness and precision he appreciated in their drawings. He even painted as they did, in flat colour, without shadows or gradations of tone. In the *Bedroom* and *Les Alyscamps,* particularly, the Japanese tendency is still further

PORTRAIT OF THE ARTIST. 1889. NATIONAL GALLERY, OSLO

stressed by the aerial perspective and diagonal composition. Nor, lastly, must it be forgotten that it was the study of Japanese prints which led to his abandonment of the 'dark' style. They had opened his eyes to the world of colour he was to find so dazzlingly splendid three years later. For it was undoubtedly at Arles that he discovered both his own colour and colour in general, together with its absolute expressive power and its spiritual significance. It was there that he accorded it the supreme status of an end in itself. We may remember what he said of red and green, that they symbolised the 'formidable passions of humanity'. For him cobalt was the 'divine colour' and solar radiation comparable with 'personal ardour'. Colour had begun by exciting his senses. It soon enhanced his mysticism and poetic feeling. 'Expression of the love of two lovers through the marriage of two complementaries, their mingling and opposition, the mysterious vibrations of tones brought into relation. Expression of thought on a face by the radiance of bright on dark.' He notes that the Old Masters, Rembrandt, Vermeer and Franz Hals, could avail themselves of shadow, chiaroscuro and value, whereas now colour could replace such artifices.

Colour was the reason for Vincent's deep admiration for Delacroix and Monticelli. Colour sent him into ecstasies before the sun, orchards in bloom, shining cornfields, the zouave's or the postman's uniform and the striped skirts of the young Arlesian

THE ROAD TO TARASCON. SUMMER 1888. KUNSTHAUS, ZURICH

THE ROAD TO TARASCON. MR. AND MRS. JUSTIN K. THANNHAUSER COLLECTION, NEW YORK

women. When nature did not provide enough of it, he invented his own. In this connection we may notice *Portrait of an Old Provençal Peasant*, the *All Night Café* and the *Bedroom*. For in his longing to 'express himself forcibly' he often saw the colours of his own imagination in things. He required such colours to be pure, as rich as possible, displayed on the canvas in thick compact, layers, with none of those mawkish transitional tones and cunning techniques, glossy surfaces, for instance, delicate glazing or transparent paint, which the great northern painters practised. Vincent said of them, with scorn, that 'they rely more on skilful brushwork and picturesque effect than on the desire to express something by colour alone'. He himself sometimes resorted to 'Monticellian

HILLS AT ST. RÉMY.
JUNE 1889. COLLECTION OF
MR. AND MRS. JUSTIN K.
THANNHAUSER, NEW YORK

'*My last canvas depicts mountains, with a blackish hut
among the olive-trees.*

'*I shall be told that mountains are not like that and
that some of my black contours are as thick as one's
finger. All the same, I think
it illustrates that passage in
Rod's book*—"The Sense of
Life"—*one of the very few
bits I like, about a land of
dark mountains where the
blackish huts of goatherds can
be seen and sunflowers are in
bloom.*'
Letter to Theo

168

impasto' and sometimes to thin and smooth paint. But his colour is always intense and harsh, austere in its lyricism and yet musical. His contemporaries called it violent, for they were used to the muddy mixtures of the Barbizon school or newly converted to the gaudy shimmer of impressionism. Vincent himself occasionally wondered whether his colour was not too tight and crude and referred to it as 'blackguard's painting'. But a stimulating book, a glance at a Japanese print or a stroll through the glowing country-side would soon set his doubts at rest. He would then consider his most extravagant studies his most coherent, harmonious and serene. Of the *All Night Café* he remarks ironically: 'Whatever would Monsieur Tersteeg say? He'd call it delirium tremens in full swing!' He saw no point in denying his instincts and his intelligence. 'It does me good to hit hard', he owns, with virile satisfaction.

Van Gogh is said to have been 'crazy', 'in a paroxysm', about colour. Yet these very critics surely remember the 'fauve' orgies, the dazzling, sumptuous productions of Matisse, the 'simultaneous contrasts' of Léger and Delaunay. No one dreamed of abusing such painters with epithets suggesting they were unbalanced mentally and, if the critics were at all literary, branding them as 'wild creatures enveloped in the clouds of the underworld' or 'like Icarus burned by solar fire'. When Vincent exclaims: 'What intensity of colour, what purity of air, what vibrant serenity!' it is hard to suppose him over-excited, deluded and driven out of his senses by colour. It seems more likely that he remained clear-headed for all his wonder and capable of conveying it accurately by his painting. It could only be a man from the northern mists who could respond with such vivacity and at the same time with such perfect self-control to the peculiar novelty of these sensations. Vincent's provincial colleagues, who paradoxically painted the beauty-spots of their regions with brushes steeped in academic pats of butter, may well seem odder characters than he. The pictorial extravagance imputed to him is not to be found in the works painted at Arles. On the contrary, we can admire the vigilance and care with which he orchestrates his symphonies of vermilions, yellows, Prussian blues and emerald greens, even his most brisk

CAMARGUE PEASANT. AUGUST 1888.
FORMERLY T. LAURIN COLLECTION, STOCKHOLM

allegro movements. The skill, again, with which he balances his contrasts by the interplay of cold and warm tones, and the dexterity with which he uses the complementary principle to temper too shrill a note in one place and reinforce sonority in another by the proximity of a minor tone are wholly admirable.

Here is his comment on the *Berceuse*: 'A woman in green with orange hair is brought forward against a background of green with pink flowers. The various sharps of raw pink, raw orange and raw green are softened by flats of red and green. . . . There may be an attempt in the *Berceuse* at some slight musical effect with colour.' This was not the first time Vincent had compared his painting with music. But his music is certainly not very gentle or soporific. He was the very antithesis of a charming singer. The van Gogh rhythm is almost always heavily stressed. The harmonies of the brass and the steady accentuation of the melody sound high and clear above it, with no transitional notes or graduated passages. The style is direct and openly aggressive, to the embarrassment of those who are fond of sly and perverse sentimentalities. 'A buzzing of teased colours, all the dizzy variants of light', was the opinion of Vincent given later by the insipid painter Maurice Denis. Since then we have listened to many strident voices, watched the excesses of fauvism and after them the expressionist frenzy. To-day we find, in the extreme saturation of van Gogh's tones, their bold contrasts and chromatic exchanges, the proofs of this great individualist's power of concentration, robust temperament, scorn for pedantry and adherence to his own self-made rules. It is not unprofitable to speak of musical painting in his case, if only to distinguish it from the modelled, sculptural style or that which dissolves in vibrations of light and further to indicate how it suggests brightness and darkness, nearness and distance, by means of juxtaposed colours, in other words by methods wholly and specifically pictorial. Such colours are too often taken for the automatic language of instinctive imperatives poured out indiscriminately. But in fact Vincent selects them with the greatest care and, superintends their production with as scrupulous an attention as he observes their effects on the canvas. For he was never indifferent to the quality of his tools and colours. That is yet another legend that needs to be dissipated.

In this connection a letter of April 1888 is most revealing. 'Please ask Tasset', he writes to Theo, 'for his opinion on the following question. It seems to me that the more finely a colour is powdered the more saturated with oil it becomes. Well, we're not terrifically fond of oil, of course. If one painted in the style of Monsieur Gerome and the other *trompe l'œil* photographers, no doubt one would want very finely powdered colours. But on the contrary it

YOUNG MALE PEASANT. MAY-JUNE 1889. E. SFORNI COLLECTION, FLORENCE

doesn't worry us if the canvas has a defaced look. If then, instead of powdering colours on the stone for God knows how long, it were powdered just long enough to render it tractable, without bothering so much about the minuteness of the particles, one would have fresher colours, perhaps with less tendency to blacken.' Vincent goes on to beg the manufacturer to try the experiment with certain colours, which he named. But Tasset of course did nothing of the sort. Vincent than decided to grind his own colours as soon as Gauguin arrived to help him. Meanwhile he used, especially for his picture *The Vines,* tubes sent him by Tanguy. He immediately declares: 'It's working well. I'm not troubled *in any way* by the larger grain.'

Another day he is quite shocked by Gauguin's commission of a technical heresy in his self-portrait. 'One should never draw with Prussian blue in a flesh tint.' He was just as fidgety over framing. He was fond of white frames, which have an insulating effect on very colourful paintings. He would have nothing to do with those over-elaborate, 'monstrous' frames so dear to pompous but inferior Dutch painters. 'Personally, my heart misses a beat when I order deal frames at five francs.' He also had them made in walnut, oak and chestnut, depending on the kind of painting to be framed. He took innumerable precautions even after a work was finished. After despatching his pictures to Theo he continued to worry. 'I beg you to keep the studies I've made here exposed to the air as much as possible, as they're not yet dried out properly. If they're kept shut up or in darkness the colours will deteriorate.'

All the above quotations prove that he was not, as has been asserted, disorderly, blundering and slapdash in his habits, indifferent to craftsmanship and 'trade secrets'. We are thus enabled gradually to disentangle his real personality from the romantic fable which has obscured it. There are further surprises in store. Between 1885, the year of *The Potato Eaters,* and 1888, that of the *All Night Café,* Vincent had discovered what colour could do. He had adopted it as an individual means of expression, going so far as to paint a yellow sky, red trees and orange hair. He had replaced natural light by what modern painters call pictorial light. But he had also become, during the same period, a great draughtsman, quite out

DAUDET'S WINDMILL. AUGUST 1888. V. W. VAN GOGH COLLECTION, LAREN

of the ordinary. The fascination exercised upon him by the Midi sun was equalled by that of linear purity, clarity of contour and the planes they imposed on the subject. We may remember his exclamation on first discovering the splendours of Provence. 'It's a country as beautiful as Japan!' When he notes: 'I believe in the necessity of a new art of colour', he immediately adds: 'and of drawing'. In the same way as he cites Delacroix and Monticelli for colour, he invokes such masters of linear design as Hokusai and Utamaro. Yet at the same time, so true is it that colour and design can never be separated, he extols both the use of colour in Japanese prints and the draughtsmanship of Delacroix and Monticelli. He was the first to discover, under the Marseilles master's bewildering profusion of paint, the 'superb, rich drawing . . . a day will come when his glorious *designs* will be hailed as great art'. When he

CYPRESSES BY MOONLIGHT. JUNE 1889. KUNSTHALLE, BREMEN

'This picture raises the eternal question whether we can see the whole of life or only know a hemisphere of it before death. I've no idea of the answer myself. But the sight of stars always sets me dreaming just as naïvely as those black dots on a map set me dreaming of towns and villages. Why should those points of light in the firmament, I wonder, be less accessible than the dark ones on the map of France? We take a train to go to Tarascon or Rouen and we take death to go to a star. What is certainly true about this argument is that as long as we're alive we can't visit a star any more than when we are dead we can take a train. Anyhow, I don't see why cholera, the stone, phthisis and cancer should not be heavenly modes of locomotion like ships, buses and trains here below, while if we die peacefully of old age we make the journey on foot.'   Letter to Theo

'As there's nothing against it—assuming that in the innumerable other planets and suns, lines, shapes and colours also exist—we may keep a comparatively open mind about the possibilities of painting on a higher, different level of existence, the difference being due to causes which may be no more malignant and surprising than the transformation of a grub into a butterfly or a cockchafer. The painter-

butterfly might have one of the innumerable stars to work in. They might be no more inaccessible to us after death than are the black dots on the map, standing for towns and villages, in our terrestrial life.

'Science, by which I mean scientific reasoning, looks to me like an instrument which will one day take us very far. For instance, at one time the earth was supposed to be flat. Well, so it is, even to-day, from Paris to Asnières. But that fact doesn't prevent science from proving that the earth as a whole is spherical. No one nowadays denies it. Well, nowadays, in spite of that, we are still at the stage of believing that life itself is flat, the distance from birth to death. Yet the probability is that life, too, is spherical and much more extensive and capacious than the hemisphere we know at present.' Letter to E. Bernard

recalls what Paul Mantz said of Delacroix' *The Boat of Christ*, 'I didn't know blue and green could have so terrifying an effect', he eagerly notes: 'You could say the same of Hokusai, but referring in that case to his *line*, his *drawing*!'

177

Vincent's worst anxieties were due to material disappointments. But those he felt as painter and draughtsman were his most noble. The gravest of his problems was that of matching form and colour and keeping their interactions on the same level. The problem could not be solved by copying reality 'even if colour or design were precisely reproduced'. In his own words, if it were possible to 'set down reality with its colour and everything else' all one would have would be its reflection. One would still have to paint the picture. The search for expression should proceed as much by drawing as by colouring. Cézanne was later to give utterance to a similar idea. 'Design and colour are not separate . . . when colour is at its richest, form is at its fullest.' Accordingly, when Vincent fully realised colour, his drawing changed. He made 'arbitrary' and 'forcible' use of it.

He never ceased to draw, producing not only sketches and preparatory studies but designs that were definite works of art, conceived and executed for their own sake. He left a huge quantity of them. Many have been lost. Whenever he could not afford to buy fresh canvases and paints or felt gorged with colour or exhausted by the effort of painting, he resorted to pencil or pen, the latter usually in the form of a trimmed reed. He drew in short, vigorous touches, scrawls, dots and hatching, as he walked along the roads, through orchards and across fields and gardens, coming to a halt before a farmhouse, a patch of waste land, a thicket or a clump of trees. Again and again he climbed the Montmajour rock (p. 158) to survey the Crau. Its 'distant perspectives, broad and peaceful, in horizontal lines,' reminded him of Koninck's and Ruysdael's Holland, though colour and atmosphere were very different. But one would give all the pictures by Ruysdael and Koninck for the admirable drawing produced by Vincent one fine May day in 1888. It shows the plain of the Crau, with its vineyards and cultivated lands, stretching away to infinity in ordered majesty, under a parching sun (p. 107). Human life is at a standstill, immobilised in the profound slumber of the earth. The clamour of the cities is hushed, together with the lamentations of poverty and suffering. There is peace under the heavens and in the artist's heart. Another drawing he brought back from Montmajour is, on the

BED OF SUNFLOWERS. AUGUST 1888. V. W. VAN GOGH COLLECTION, LAREN

contrary, remarkable for its note of asperity (p. 159). It represents 'masses of white rock overgrown with lichen, with sections of fallen wall scattered here and there among the greenery.' These objects are freely drawn with the point of a reed, roughly sharpened so as to give a better idea of the disorderly pattern of tangled grass and heaps of sunburned stone.

Whether he selects so complicated a subject as the sea at Les Saintes-Maries (p. 121), a village prostrate in the sun, the corner of a garden (p. 136), a bed of sunflowers (p. 179) or one so simple as a flowering stalk, the structure and authoritative lines are instantly brought out, each form differentiated, with its significant detail suggested, and isolated from its neighbour so as to restore its essence by eliminating accessory items. Yet the form is not modelled, does not 'turn away' in space or cast a shadow. Vincent takes care not to unravel its outer covering and smother it in iridescent ingenuities. There is no trace of impressionism in his drawings. Classical devices have been dropped. The distance travelled by Vincent during these few years may be estimated by a comparison of the meticulously 'finished' drawings of The Hague period and the massive, compact peasants of Nuenen, their modelling thrown into sharp relief by the interplay of half-tones, as well as the analytical Parisian landscapes (p. 75), with his Arles designs. Drawing no longer meant for him pointless imitation, the irresolute definition of forms in blacks and whites softened by the tone-scale. He now boldly stripped objects of their temporary appearances and, accentuated particular elements of them, revealing the skeleton and the characteristic detail which differentiated each from all the rest.

He thus accumulated an extensive vocabulary of symbols and an extremely flexible syntax. Closely adjacent parallels suggest shadow, empty space light and a multitude of straight lines pointing in all directions define the three dimensions (cf. *Roofs*, p. 89). His clean, free line may be prolonged, without a break, in graceful inflections, as in the amazing drawing entitled *Banks of the Rhône* (p. 131). Or it may be knotted in a tangled skein of boughs and threadlike twigs, as in *Provençal Orchard* (p. 91). Or again it may break up into short dashes, straight, flexed or scribbled, as in

VINCENT'S ROOM. SEPTEMBER 1889. V. W. VAN GOGH COLLECTION, LAREN

*'I've done . . . a canvas of my bedroom. It has deal furniture, as you know.
It amused me enormously to paint the bare, Seurat-like simplicity of such an
interior. The colours are flat but laid on in rough impasto, the walls, pale lilac,
the floor in broken, faded reds, the chairs and bedstead chrome yellow, with the
pillows and sheet a very pale lemon green, the coverlet blood-red, while the dressing-
table is orange, the wash-basin blue and the window green. I wanted to suggest
absolute repose, you see, by all these disparate tones, the only touch of white being
provided by the black-framed mirror, this passage constituting the fourth pair of
complementaries in the painting.'* Letter to Gauguin

Garden Corner (p. 110) or *View of Arles*. In *Provençal Farmhouse*
(p. 127) and *Cornfield* (p. 143) a few swift strokes, widely spaced,
give the illusion of a motionless land sunk in the torpor of
summer. Moreover, bearing in mind that the primary feeling of the
draughtsman is for colour, we may note how, in *The Sower* (p. 194)

181

and better still in *Landscape with Telegraph Poles* (p. 146), the intense blue of the sky is rendered by a collection of dots and its complementary colour by the paper itself, where only a few scrawled commas indicate the nature of the ground.

Lastly, one of Vincent's greatest achievements was the substitution of an "invented" for classic space, the former obeying laws different from those of monocular vision with its lines running to the horizon. Study of the drawing called *The Washerwomen* reveals that the background landscape is sketched in conformity with traditional perspective, while the canal and its banks are seen from above (p. 151). In this work, accordingly, so unusual for its period —1888—two angles of vision are juxtaposed, affording a simultaneous representation of two spaces in reality successive. It is clear that in this distortion of nature Vincent introduces a new notion, that of time. His interpretation of the world is not tactile like that of Cézanne. Nor is it, like Gauguin's, reduced to two dimensions. It is synthetic and polyvalent, opposed to the refined analytical system of Claude Monet, which weakens contour to suggest the flight of time. Vincent's innovation is not disconcerting, for his heterogeneous spaces are unified by the spirit in which they have been so closely associated.

In any case, although the artist worked from inspiration in these drawings, nothing in them is left to chance. All is the result of mature reflection and preparation. Whether Vincent uses the pen, the pencil or the reed, charcoal, ink or lead, whether or not he heightens the effect with water-colour, all the designs bear the imprint of a powerfully organised personality. The tension and authority of the style are most remarkable, as is the frank and resolute way in which he develops his style unhesitatingly to its confident, vibrant climax under a hand steady as a rock. 'It was all done by temperament', Emile Bernard wrote later. 'There was no cold calculation, simply the sure intuition of deep emotion and an ardent spirit.' But Vincent's art arose not only from temperament but also from the intention to speak out on deliberately controlled lines in accordance with highly practical technical requirements. He was eminently capable of restraining his ardour by his intelligence, curbing his impatience, managing a plunging pencil and aiming for

GARDEN WITH THISTLES. OCTOBER 1888. V. W. VAN GOGH COLLECTION, LAREN

a bull's-eye. These are some of his best drawings, among the finest in modern art. But if we compare drawing with painting in the cases of the *Zouave* (p. 154), the *Postman Roulin* and the *Mousmé*, we shall find that, though the first of these portraits is so expert that each line of the drawing is precisely repeated by the brush, the *Mousmé* painting, admirable as it is, remains inferior to the drawing (p. 108), while the postman has less power and distinction on the paper than he has on the canvas (p. 116).

For the sake of analysis we have separated elements, colour and design, which in Vincent are inseparable. For him each form has a colour and each colour a form. It was at Arles that he first stopped sketching his subject in charcoal and 'embarked on drawing with colour itself'. It is true that Delacroix, Manet, Renoir and Monticelli also drew in the act of painting. Yet while they saw their

HOSPITAL GROUNDS
AT ST. RÉMY. OCTOBER 1889.
FOLKWANG MUSEUM, ESSEN

'This is a view of the grounds of the private hospital where I am living. Grey terrace to the right, with a section of the building. A few withered rose-bushes, with the grounds on the left, red ochre, parched by the sun and covered with fallen fir-twigs. . . . The first tree has an enormous trunk, but it has been struck by lightning and sawn. Nevertheless, one of the side branches shoots up very high and bends down again in an avalanche of dark green twigs. This grim giant, an image of humbled pride, contrasts, if we consider the tree as a living being, with the pallid smile of a last rose on the fading bush facing it. . . . The sky is reflected in yellow, after the rain, in a puddle. A sunbeam, the last, raises the dim ochre tone to orange.

'You will understand that this combination of red ochre, green rendered melancholy by grey and black contour lines illustrates to some extent the feeling of anguish that often afflicts some of my companions in misfortune, known as "black-red". The idea is reinforced, incidentally, by the theme of the big tree struck by lightning and the sickly, greenish-pink smile of the last autumn flower.'
Letter to E. Bernard

185

forms as dissolved in chiaroscuro, in the atmosphere, or fragmented by impasto brushwork, Vincent detaches his own from their shadows, seizing upon them with fierce eagerness to range them in his elliptical and subdivided composition. His colours achieve their magic through his extremely expressive and original language of drawing. He is quite frank about his method. 'Though I always work direct on to the canvas, I try first to note what is essential in the design, then the spaces enclosed by the contours and always felt, whether expressed or not. In every case I give them tones simplified to the same extent, by which I mean that everything representing ground receives the same tone of violet, the whole sky a blue tone, greenery either a bluish or yellowish green, the yellow or blue qualities being deliberately exaggerated in that case. In short, I never allow *trompe l'œil* anywhere.'

One always feels that the Arles painter draws while he paints. Every touch of colour is at the same time an expressive stroke or line. Nothing is imitated. All is creation and evocation. The brush darts and slashes, flicks, stabs and skims, wrestling with form, striking out the volume and tearing gaps for a sudden revelation of depth. Patterns like ears of corn or swarms of bacilli, hatchings and dots, are more or less compressed to indicate fading light. Their length, thickness and direction are altered to stress the slope of a ravine or a rocky peak, the inclination of a brow or the base of a neck, to distinguish a cedar from a pine, a field of cut swathes from the surge of ripe corn or one face from another. No artist ever had such a varied collection of brush-strokes. He could set them like splinters in the quick of his paint and immediately afterwards gash the canvas with a virulent jet of colour. He could blend them in a sprawling impasto, break them up further on into jerky angularities or wind them in ribbons of fire around the sun or a lamp. In the portraits they seem to build up the subject by a series of jolts. In the landscapes they often extend into flowing undulations and in his later period, after his hand had grown feverish under hallucination, they curl round cypresses, whirl almost audibly upwards to the clouds and twine in spirals, ringlets and scarves among gyrating stars. A few splashes of colour are enough to indicate the framework and aspect of a form, notably in the

GARDEN IN PROVENCE. 1889. V. W. VAN GOGH COLLECTION, LAREN

Self-Portrait with a Straw Hat, *Moored Boats* and *Haystacks in Wet Weather* (Cat. 124). On the other hand strokes are multiplied, collected in battalions, for the assault of ploughland, a cornfield (cf. *Summer Evening Near Arles*), a mass of greenery, as in the *Poet's Garden* or a flower-bed. But he could equally well renounce this wealth of resources to express with the minimum of means the oceanic calm of nature or his own humility as rendered in the humblest objects, clogs, shoes, a true-trunk or a chair.

Many of his canvases, fascinating as they still are, give only a faint idea of their original state, when their raw colours horrified the Parisian aesthetes. We have already noted what vigilant precautions Vincent took in choosing his paints. Unfortunately chemistry at that time had not reached its present stage of development. His lakes have evaporated. His chromes and Veronese greens have become oxidised. His Prussian blue and flake white have darkened, absorbing the colours with which they were mixed. Many of his works have therefore lost their pristine brilliance. Tonal relations have been falsified and deteriorate from year to year. But even when only pale reflections of his masterpieces in oil remain, his drawings will still be unreservedly admired. It is already being recognised that his genius is most clearly evident on such sheets of paper, otherwise untouched. People are beginning to wonder whether he was not an even greater draughtsman than he was a painter.

WHEN Gauguin knocked at his door on the 20th October 1888 Vincent was feeling exhausted. Eight months of frenzied work had disorganised his physique. But the arrival of his friend, so long awaited and so often postponed owing to the pressing debts which Theo had eventually managed to settle, revived van Gogh's enthusiasm. He had furnished and decorated the yellow house in honour of his guest. His isolation had been ended and his dream realised. In Gauguin, 'my friend Gauguin', now at Arles with him and sharing the same roof, he saw a companion for the winter and a promising start for the 'Midi Studio'. Surely the 'others' wouldn't hesitate to come now. Gauguin would be head of the school. So Vincent, then under his influence, had decided. The painter from Pont Aven in Brittany was prompt to take active command. He put the house in order, checked daily expenditure, organised work and relaxation, even the nocturnal expeditions, the rounds of absinthe in the cafés and the erotic exploits with the girls of the Bout d'Arles quarter. He also took intellectual charge of the Studio. Gauguin's character was authoritative and arrogant. After holding court at Pont Aven and having only recently acquired the prestige which his discovery of the 'synthetic' method had conferred on him, he now proceeded to assuage his thirst for domination by giving orders to Vincent. The relation between the two, owing to Gauguin's prodigality in proffering theories and advice and his intolerance of contradiction, resembled that of master and pupil rather than reciprocal friendship. Vincent, with his constant

CHIEF SUPERINTENDENT OF ST. PAUL'S HOSPITAL. SEPTEMBER 1889.
MME. G. DUBI-MÜLLER COLLECTION, SOLEURE

tendency to humble and sacrifice himself, submitted willingly to the discipline imposed. He listened with docility at first to Gauguin's haughty and confident lectures on pictorial symbolism, the partitioning of form, the intellectual value of line, the necessity of broad areas of colour and decorative arrangement.

It was under Gauguin's imperious influence that Vincent painted the *Woman Reading* (p. 144), the portrait of *Madame Roulin and her Baby* (Cat. 154) that of her eldest son *Armand* (Cat. 155), her younger son *Camille* and that of the three months old *Baby*. He forced himself to 'partition' form, govern his line and unify his planes. Ornamental arabesque appears even in the *Berceuse* (Cat. 160). But the result was not always happy. The *Dance Hall*, the *Sands* and the *Arles Promenade* are in fact failures. It is true that they were the first works which Vincent, after being put through his paces by Gauguin, painted without the subject before him. The *Promenade at Arles* (Cat. 152) was actually sheer invention. Memories of the family garden at Etten are combined with purely Provençal elements. In this work, even more than in the others, he schooled himself to apply the 'synthesist' technique. He systematically marked out zones of colour, flattened volume and, drew sinuous curves, with a plunging perspective and no horizon. He even resorted to an expedient dear to Gauguin and Emile Bernard by placing figures in strong relief in a corner of the foreground so as to stress depth in the rest of the composition.

Van Gogh was naturally delighted to show Gauguin round Arles and take him to such favourite haunts as the Station Café painted two months previously as the *All Night Café*. It was there that the two artists, one day in November, asked the manageress to come to their table and pose for them a moment. As Vincent worked, his companion, looking over his shoulder, kept saying: 'Madame Ginoux, your portrait will be hung in the Louvre in Paris.' Gauguin was right. This portrait was in fact hung in the Louvre some years ago. Gauguin also made a drawing of Madame Ginoux, which he used a few days later in his painting of *The Arles Café*, now in Moscow. In van Gogh's picture, called *L'Arlésienne*, Madame Ginoux is shown seated with her elbows on a table, where there are also gloves and an umbrella. Three other

I heard Rodin had a beautiful
head at the Salon.
I have been to the seaside for a
week and very likely am going thither
again soon. — Flat shore ~~sands~~
sands — fine figures there
like Cimabue — straight stylish
I am working at a Sower.

The great field all violet. The sky & sun very
yellow. It is a hard subject to treat.
Please remember me very kindly to
Mrs Russell — and in thought I heartily
shake hands.   yours very truly
                                    Vincent

LETTER TO JOHN RUSSELL. JUNE-JULY 1888.
MR. AND MRS. JUSTIN K. THANNHAUSER COLLECTION, NEW YORK

JEAN-FRANCOIS MILLET. THE SOWER. 1850.
MUSEUM OF FINE ARTS, BOSTON

versions of the painting exist, in which books are substituted for
the gloves and umbrella. By far the best is in the Metropolitan
Museum of New York (Cat. 153). It was also painted in November
1888. The other two copies date from 1889 and were made at St
Rémy (Cat. 193).

THE SOWER (AFTER MILLET). NOVEMBER 1889-JANUARY 1890.
COLLECTION OF MR. AND MRS. MORRIS W. HAFT, NEW YORK

Gauguin was still with Vincent when he painted the *Red Vines* (p. 145). But this picture is entirely self-executed and self-inspired. The vines are purple in the light of the setting sun. The sky is saffron, the ground violet, with some scattered blue forms of women gathering grapes. The river on the right sends up varied

THE SOWER. AUGUST 1880.
V. W. VAN GOGH COLLECTION, LAREN

THE SOWER. SEPTEMBER 1881.
PRIVATE COLLECTION, DELFT

THE SOWER. JUNE 1888. V. W. VAN GOGH COLLECTION, LAREN

THE SOWERS. SEPTEMBER 1881.
V. W. VAN GOGH COLLECTION, LAREN

PEASANT SOWING. SEPTEMBER 1881.
KRÖLLER-MÜLLER RIJKSMUSEUM, OTTERLO

SOWERS AND STUDIES OF HANDS. 1890. V. W. VAN GOGH COLLECTION, LAREN

reflections of gold and silver. The light is fiery, yet mellow. All these features combine in the exceptional quality of the picture, the only one of all Vincent's works which was bought in his life-time. It is obvious that as soon as Vincent returned to direct contact with reality he instantly recovered his creative power. He realised the fact himself, to the extent of finding Gauguin's tuition less and less endurable. Symbolist aesthetics ˙ and decorative abstraction, forced upon him more and more insistently day by day, could hardly be reconciled with his profoundest aspirations. Consequently, after the first brief enthusiasm, he felt that his personal integrity and convictions were being endangered. Annoyance was soon followed by positive revolt. The two men came into conflict, Gauguin presuming upon his authority and Vincent no longer obeying him. They disagreed about everything, including their habits and tastes. One could not, of course, imagine people more dissimilar. Disputes and quarrels broke out on all sorts of subjects. Van Gogh indeed, with his customary clear-headedness, had long since seen through Gauguin. He had recognised in the former bank-clerk the coldly calculating and matter of fact individualist and egotist, interested only, as an artist, in carving out a brilliant and lucrative career for himself. In several letters written to Theo during the previous summer he had made no secret of his view of Gauguin. But in his whole-hearted devotion to the chimerical project of the 'Midi Studio' he paid no attention to his instinctive distrust of the man. He was determined to have Gauguin with him at all costs. He was ready for any concession, any sacrifice, if only the yellow house could be made a centre for work in common. In a letter to Gauguin dated the 8th October 1888 he offered to put him in charge of the future studio, urging him in positively abject terms to make up his mind to come. 'I find my own artistic ideas excessively commonplace in comparison with yours. I have always had the coarse appetites of a brute.'

Vincent was blinded for the time being by his delight at Gauguin's arrival. But the illusion did not last. He saw that he had made a mistake and that his dream was in ruins. He then felt as forsaken as an empty shell by the seashore. He knew he would go on struggling, but without energy or conviction, except the convic-

PEASANTS AT WORK (AFTER MILLET). APRIL 1890. COLLECTION OF
MR. AND MRS. JUSTIN K. THANNHAUSER, NEW YORK

tion that all was lost now. He had hoped to be able to share all that
he believed in and loved, which others had been too timid or too
self-centred to accept from him, with an artist like himself, misunderstood, fighting the same battle and worshipping the same
divinity. But that artist, the prospective companion and brother,
had not responded. In reality it could not have been otherwise.
Vincent forgot that great creative spirits are as little suited to
understand one another as the heroes of tragedy. The stronger
their personalities are, the less inclined they feel to pool their
researches. Each goes his own way separately from the other,
sometimes in opposition to him. Such is the explanation of the disagreements between Gauguin and Vincent, which soon led to the

197

rupture of their association. To the former it was a mere episode, to the latter an irreparable disaster. He did not survive it. The revolver bullet which ended his life was in reality, though quite involuntarily, fired by Gauguin.

The long months of intensive work and insufficient food rendered Vincent less capable than Gauguin, who was the stronger and tougher, of resisting the inroads of habitual absinthe drinking and erotic debauchery. Alcohol, and still more contradiction, affected his nerves. One day they both visited the Bruyas collection in the Montpellier museum. They returned embittered and dissatisfied with each other. More wrangling ensued. Vincent became deeply depressed. He could understand Gauguin's boredom with Arles and contempt for the yellow house and his own host. But he could not bear Gauguin's derision of the 'Midi Studio' and preparations to wreck it by precipitate departure. For Gauguin seemed to have quite decided to break off the association on which the other had staked not only his hopes but his very salvation. The coming separation haunted Vincent to such an extent that he conveyed his feelings in two most touching canvases. The first represents a yellow chair standing on a red-tiled floor (p. 148), the second a red and green armchair. They were Vincent's and Gauguin's respectively, for of course Gauguin occupied the most comfortable of the two. On the first chair lay a pipe and a screw of tobacco, on the second two books and a lighted candle (Cat. 157). 'I tried to paint his empty place', Vincent wrote later to Albert Aurier, referring to the armchair. His own chair, too, was empty. Such was the way in which this sensitive and guileless man prefigured his existence once his companion had left him. There would be two pictures side by side in the lonely room, two empty chairs, symbols of an ended friendship, the broken ties between two people whose habits were indicated by the books and the candle, the pipe and the screw of tobacco. The chairs expressed a great deal more than their characters as objects. They meant regret, solitude, absence. They were absence itself. 'Rather curious' studies Vincent was to call them later, with a heavy heart. But the fact is that no painter has ever conveyed so much, or such poignant grief, by means of such simple objects and in a style of such deep humility.

THE STONE BENCH IN THE HOSPITAL GARDENS. MAY 1889.
V. W. VAN GOGH COLLECTION, LAREN

TREE-TRUNKS. MAY 1890.
KRÖLLER-MÜLLER
RIJKSMUSEUM, OTTERLO

'*Work is going on well. I've
done two canvases of the fresh
grass in the park. One of
them is very simple. Here's a
quick sketch of it. There is a
violet and pink fir trunk,
some grass with white flowers
and dandelions, a little rose-
tree and some other tree-
trunks in the background,
right at the top of the canvas.*'
Letter to Theo

Gauguin, accordingly, soon departed, leaving behind him an inconsolable friend, an exhausted body and a disordered brain. But we can forgive Gauguin. Everyone knows how egotistically and cruelly artists may behave when their independence is at stake. Van Gogh is the only exception. His good nature, tolerance and altruism were inexhaustible, no doubt because he was something more than an artist.

On the 23rd December Vincent informed his brother that Gauguin was sick of the pleasant town of Arles, the little yellow house and above all of Vincent himself. Next day, if we may believe Gauguin, Vincent threw his glass in his friend's face during a quarrel. On Christmas morning Gauguin made his preparations to leave and that evening he took his departure, alone. But he soon heard hasty, irregular footsteps behind him. Turning round, he saw Vincent coming at him with a razor. Gauguin gave him a steady stare. Vincent stopped, then turned and fled back to his room, where he locked the door and cut off the lobe of his left ear. Wrapping it in a handkerchief, he rushed to a brothel in the Bout d'Arles quarter and offered the severed lobe to Rachel, one of the girls there. Then he returned home, went to bed and fell into a profound slumber. The next morning Gauguin, who had spent the night at a hotel, saw a crowd outside the yellow house. The police had just found Vincent lying unconscious on his bed among towels stained with blood. On coming to himself he called for Gauguin. But the latter had disappeared. Vincent was taken to hospital, where he became so hysterically violent that he had to be placed in a cell for dangerous lunatics.

There is no need to invoke complex scientific ideas for an explanation of this tragedy. It was the logical consequence of all that we already know of this unhappy man. Gauguin had failed him. He had always been terrified of being left alone. His dream had collapsed. The 'Midi Studio' would henceforth be beyond his reach. In addition to the extreme over-excitement following upon a long period of privation he had been working himself to a standstill and drinking heavily. It was no wonder that the cord had been stretched past breaking point. We have to imagine his state of mind when Gauguin announced his departure. In this fresh

THE FOUNTAIN IN THE GARDEN OF THE HOSPITAL AT ST. RÉMY. MAY 1889.
V. W. VAN GOGH COLLECTION, LAREN

defeat he had the appalling sensation of having been outlawed by
that very humanity with which he had always longed, from childhood, to be united. This inferiority complex was reinforced by one
of guilt. Like Orestes turning, in his mania, upon himself, he
punishes his guilt by severing his own ear. Next, in a Christian
spirit of self-sacrifice he carries this fragment of himself, his own
living flesh, to the most fallen of human beings.

The most astonishing feature of this tragic sequence of events is that its central figure did not break down sooner. If his constitution had been less robust, overwork and the excessive strain on his nerves would have brought his hereditary psychosis to a head much earlier. It eventually struck down Theo in his turn with far less reason. In any case, after three days of acute delirium, accompanied by aural and visual hallucinations, the 'robust' Vincent came to his senses and turned to survey, with a courage and serenity equally remarkable, the ruins of his life. Meanwhile Gauguin had returned to Paris after sending a telegram to Theo. Vincent, on his recovery, was grieved to hear that his brother had rushed to Arles but already left again, reassured by the house-surgeon Félix Rey, the same doctor who afterwards attended Vincent so conscientiously. On the 1st January 1889 the patient wrote a soothing letter to Theo and also 'a few words of sincere and profound friendship' to Gauguin. In this letter, an infinitely sad one, there is no trace of rancour or reproach and only the mildest of allusions to recent events. 'Tell me, was my brother's journey really so necessary?'

Thanks to the devotion in all respects of Félix Rey, Vincent regained his health. When he left the hospital on the 7th January 1889 no one had any reason to suppose that he was not completely sane once more. Moreover, according to the statement of Dr. Rey, reported by Drs. Leroy and Doiteau, it was before Vincent left the hospital that he painted the admirable picture called *The Hospital at Arles*, now in the Reinhart collection (Cat. 159). His illness, therefore had been brief. On the 9th January he learned that Theo had gone to Amsterdam for his betrothal to Johanna Bonger. He was reassured by the news, for he had feared that his indisposition might prevent his brother taking this step. But Vincent had other troubles. After paying his debts he found he was penniless. Consequently, he had to undergo 'a most rigorous fast'. Moreover, his good-natured and loyal friend, the postman Roulin, was about to leave Arles on being promoted to a higher post in Marseilles. Vincent dreaded the loneliness which this excellent man's departure would mean for him. He was sleeping badly and suffering from nightmares. Nevertheless, he resumed work.

SCHOOLBOY. JANUARY 1890. MUSEUM OF ART, SAO PAULO

When he looked in the mirror he saw an emaciated countenance, surgical dressing over the mutilated ear, a fur cap on the head and a thick jacket buttoned over the chest to keep out the cold. He proceeded to paint *Man with Severed Ear* (p. 160) and a further self-portrait, *Man with Pipe* (p. 161), which innumerable reproductions have made famous all over the world. It is obvious that so masterly a painting could not have been executed by anyone whose mind was at all unbalanced. The firmness of the drawing, strong colour and extreme simplicity of handling combine to give an impression of vigour and serenity at which Vincent had no doubt aimed. The effect would have been fully obtained if it had not been for the disturbing stare of the intensely blue blue eyes, which seem to miss nothing and yet see nothing. His next portrait was that of *Doctor Rey* (Cat. 163), who was still attending him. The energetic and smiling features of the subject have been penetratingly observed and recorded, the likeness caught by a sure hand. Forms have been outlined and volume emphasised with equal certainty, as well as the violent, harsh colouring resembling that of crude popular illustration. The same confidence is evident in the placing against the green background of the ornamental spiral and lozenge shapes closely related to the inflections of the sitter's shoulders and facial rotundities. This remarkable portrait is also the living image of the stability and optimism then cultivated by van Gogh as an antidote to the malady from which he had so narrowly escaped. He resumed a study he had made of Madame Roulin in December 1888, the *Berceuse* (Cat. 160), making three successive versions of it. It was also in the January days following his discharge from hospital that he produced a series of still-life paintings, representing his drawing-board with some onions and other objects (Cat. 161), a basket of fruit with a pair of gloves (Cat. 162), flowers in a vase (Cat. 164), a pair of clogs and crabs on a table. A man whose mind was affected could hardly have produced so considerable a body of excellent work. By the end of January, moreover, he was writing to tell Theo that he felt quite well again, adding: 'I'm amazed to find how keen I am on working.' But this blaze of zeal soon died down. It was followed by prostration. Symptoms of delirium and hallucination suddenly set in. On the 6th or 7th of February Dr. Rey ordered his return to hospital.

When, some days later, he regained consciousness, he could no longer ignore the cruel truth. The hysterical fit in December had not been an accident, a passing weakness. He had henceforth to reckon with the secret enemy within that threatened to destroy him. In spite of his discouragement he picked up his brushes again

THE CORNFIELD. JUNE 1889. G. SERIGIERS COLLECTION, BRUSSELS

on the 22nd February to start a fourth version of the *Berceuse*. But his continual resumptions of this theme were never wholly satisfactory, though he had once been able to 'hack out' a masterpiece in three-quarters of an hour. When the door of his dark cell was opened and he returned to the sunlit city and the landscape coloured like a dream from the 'Thousand and One Nights' which had filled him almost daily with happy zest a year earlier, he could only feel depression. Life seemed to him as cold and empty as his studio. During his absence no one had lit a fire in the house. It had been flooded. The walls dripped with humidity and several of his studies had been ruined by the damp. He wrote to Theo: 'Not only has the idea of the Studio foundered but even the studies which would have reminded me of it have been spoilt. The blow

has been so decisive and yet I longed so much to start something
very simple but lasting!' Nor did he feel that he had any right to
repeat so unfortunate an experiment, for there was no guarantee
that he would not have a relapse and the next crisis might be
worse than its predecessors. Yet the vicious circle to which he
appeared doomed was intolerable to him. He did not believe he
could be cured, shaken as he knew himself to be to the very depths
of his spirit. Even if he could suppose that his psychosis would
allow him some intervals of normality, it was almost bound to

GUSTAVE DORÉ. PRISONERS AT EXERCISE. 1872

PRISONERS AT EXERCISE (AFTER DORÉ). FEBRUARY 1890.
PUSHKIN MUSEUM, MOSCOW

CYPRESSES. JUNE 1889. BROOKLYN MUSEUM, NEW YORK

return with increased violence at any time. Then he would 'lose his head'. And as in spite of all he still retained his common sense, he wondered whether it would not be best to retire to an asylum. He faced this possibility with courage. But he would make one condition. The step was not to be taken without his prior knowledge. His dignity as 'painter and workman' must be respected. His acceptance of eventual incarceration was dictated by the most noble of sentiments, consideration for others, unselfish resignation, the altruistic vocation which led him to desire that his malady should not become a burden to anyone else. He analysed his case with almost terrifying penetration. 'So often,' he exclaims, 'I feel perfectly normal.' As though to prove the statement, he started new drawings and paintings.

In March 1889 he made a study of the *Postman Roulin* (Cat. 165), who had come to spend a Sunday at Arles. Next he painted the Crau peachtrees in bloom (Cat. 166) and parts of various orchards in their white and pink garb of spring. It was the second time he had seen the fairyland of spring in Provence. But now the gaiety, the 'prodigious pleasure', it had given him the year before was absent. Painting had come to be a counter-measure, occupational therapy, a way of overcoming the anguish that tormented him. Work was henceforth a moral necessity. His scruples returned in even greater force. 'You've always impoverished yourself to keep me going', he wrote to Theo. 'But I'll pay you back or die in the attempt.' He could have found a retreat better suited to his condition than Arles. But he hated the idea of leaving the town, though its 'good people', heaven knows, gave him little cause to be pleased with them. They all regarded him with spiteful curiosity, watching him in the street with mingled hostility and fear. To them he seemed a crazy dauber, dressed like a beggar, the contemptible central figure of a scandal, the man who had once used a razor against himself and might one day turn it against honest men. There were shouts of 'Look at the madman!' The children threw stones at him and followed him home. The poor man, in his exasperation at so much folly and malice, sometimes retorted to the insults offered him. Eventually a petition signed by eighty-one of the inhabitants of Arles, demanding the permanent incarceration of the artist, was addressed to the mayor. 'Those virtuous cannibals', as Vincent called them later, succeeded in their application. He was taken to hospital and placed in a cell. His house was officially sealed.

He was allowed out on the 24th March, for the day only, at the request of the painter Signac, who had specially come to Arles to see him. Before the impressionist master left, Vincent presented him with one of his recent canvases, *Still Life with Smoked Herrings*. This visit did van Gogh a lot of good. He felt a new 'desire and taste for work'. But he could do little in the hospital, where he was kept locked up, under constant supervision. He thought sadly of the gardens in bloom, the budding countryside and the glorious sun that shone for free men. He longed to return to them. But doubts assailed him. 'Shall I ever be able to build soundly on the foundations of so undermined and battered a past?' The question is followed by a phrase of heart-rending resignation. 'I feel inclined to accept outright my position as a madman, like Degas pretending to be a solicitor.' He was eventually allowed to go to the yellow house for his painting materials and a few of his favourite books, by Dostoievksy, Tolstoy, Flaubert and Renan. He began a fifth version of the *Berceuse*. But his heart was not in the work. He brooded over the past three months, with their recurrent 'indescribable moral torments' and fleeting moments of hope. He recalled the epitaph on an ancient tomb at Carpentras in the Department of Vaucluse. 'Thebe, daughter of Thelhui, priestess of Osiris, who never complained of anyone.' He wished, with a sigh, that he had 'enough good sense, patience and serenity to become like the estimable Thebe.' With a humility beyond the capacity of man to maintain he swore that in future he would blame no one but himself for his misfortunes.

Yet he wrote to Theo at the beginning of April: 'I'm feeling well these days, except for a certain background of vague melancholy, difficult to define—but anyhow I've rather improved than deteriorated physically and I'm working.' He was in fact going out every day to paint in the orchards. Now that he had been ejected from his studio he was distinctly apprehensive of the idea of making a new life for himself anywhere else, where he would be entirely isolated. After all, why should he not remain permanently at the Arles asylum, where he would have the company of other patients to distract him? If the worst came to the worst he would consent to leave it for that of St. Rémy, of which he had heard. He felt sufficiently attracted by the idea to write: 'I have asked for arrangements to be made to transfer me there, as a boarder under super-

THE FENCED FIELD. APRIL 1890. KRÖLLER-MÜLLER RIJKSMUSEUM, OTTERLO

vision, at the end of this month or the beginning of May.' It had certainly not been without a pang of misgiving that he had himself decided to request confinement. For 'the weather is fine and the sun glorious'. Just as he had a year ago, he was drawing and painting in the gardens, in the midst of the increasing greenery of the countryside, among the flowering trees. With the exception of the *View of Arles* (Cat. 167), with its gnarled tree-trunks in the foreground, rows of peach-trees in bloom in the middle distance and the houses of the town in the background, the pictures of this period, for instance *The Old Willows* (Cat. 169), are rather clumsily and slackly painted. It is evident that the artist has ceased to feel the wonder and joyous ecstasy recorded in the great series of canvases produced in the spring of 1888.

While Theo was getting married in Holland, Vincent was clearing his studio for the move to St. Rémy. Alas for the 'Studio of the Future'! He stored his furniture in a room at the 'All Night Café' and packed up his pictures for despatch to his brother, describing the process of liquidation to him as follows: 'I felt it deeply, especially because you had given me all that stuff with such brotherly generosity and yet it was you alone who continued to support me for so many years till in the end I could only report this miserable outcome of it all. . . . Your kindness to me has not been wasted. You showed it and it remains part of you and always will, all the more if it never brings in any material profit. But I can't express my feelings properly.'

It was a confession of failure. He went on to state his repentance.

'Don't grieve over it. . . .' Theo is not to blame himself for his brother's privations due to inadequate help. Over-smoking and over-drinking, Vincent writes, had contributed to his mental breakdown. He protests that one can't possess all the virtues. Since all Theo's generosity and self-sacrifice had been in vain, he should transfer to his wife the affection hitherto lavished on his brother. Vincent adds that he is going to try hard himself to come to terms with his distracted mentality and console himself if possible with a little more painting and drawing, 'less frantically than I did last year'.

He has heard that he will be forbidden to work at St. Rémy. Well, that remained to be seen. In any case it will be better for him to be under supervision than left to himself, all the more so since 'that head of mine is by no means yet quite what it ought to be'. But we must not suppose that he had lost even a fraction of his faculties. The very fact that he analysed and reflected on his case proves that he had not. There are even moments when his inspiration raises him above his affliction and worries. 'My dear Theo, if you could only see the olive-trees just now! The leaves are like old silver, with a greenish tinge against the blue. And the orange tints of the ploughed fields!' A poetic passage follows. 'There is a kind of intensely confidential utterance, that seems immemorially ancient, in the whispers of an olive-orchard. It's too beautiful for me to dare to paint or even imagine it. And the oleander is the very

CORNFIELD IN THE ALPILLES. JUNE 1889. V. W. VAN GOGH COLLECTION, LAREN

voice of love!' He could not bear to think that he must not yield to all these temptations. For the cost of painting was high and his own had already cost him quite enough. The most important thing for the time being was for him to enter a mental home as a boarder. The charge at St. Rémy was a hundred francs a month. Would Theo, now that he was married and had more expenses, still be able to help? Vincent appealed to him in desperation. 'If I had not your affection I should be driven remorselessly to suicide. Coward as I am, I should end by committing it.' Theo answered that he would pay the boarding charge. 'It'll be all right about St. Rémy.' On the 3rd May the pastor Salles, who had been very kind to him during the last few weeks, escorted him to the St. Paul-de-Mausole asylum. Vincent was fated to remain there a year.

THE PLAIN, AUVERS. ABOUT 24 JUNE 1890. KUNSTHISTORISCHES MUSEUM, VIENNA

THE director of the asylum, a former naval surgeon named Peyron, put a small room on the ground floor at the disposal of his new boarder. The sight of the lunatics in this 'menagerie', with their weird behaviour, and the sound of their shrieks at night, far from intimidating Vincent, engaged his compassion. After all, mania was a disease like any other. And the lunatics, when they were not having their fits, were reasonable beings, even capable of friendship. Vincent liked his room. Through the barred window he could see 'a square, walled cornfield, with a view like one of Van Goyen's. I can watch the sun rise over it in all his glory every morning.'

He was allowed to work. He at once began four pictures of the irises (Cat. 170) and a lilac-bush in the garden, going on to paint great tree-trunks covered with ivy in the neglected grounds of the asylum. He drew a lawn, various plants, a stone bench (p. 199) the fountain in the garden and a large, rather rare moth called the 'death's head'. He would have liked to paint it, but gave up the idea, for his pity extended to the lowest forms of life. 'It would have been necessary to kill the insect. That would have been a shame, it was so beautiful.' He painted it from memory, however, a few days later.

When he was not drawing or painting, he read, at this period mostly Balzac and Dickens. To be shut up with lunatics did not disturb him in the least. For a whole month he had no wish to go anywhere else. It was true that he had plenty to do. He wrote, referring to his companions in misfortune: 'I find it hard to understand their utter idleness.' He continued to correspond with his brother, putting innumerable questions about the pictures sent to Theo. How were the *Sunflowers* and the *Berceuse* being framed? The latest canvases should be nailed on wooden supports, the *Bedroom* should be stretched and the very dry pictures washed in water and alcohol to remove excess oil and turpentine. He repeatedly discussed the books he was reading and his favourite artists such as Rembrandt, Hals, Delacroix, Daumier, Rousseau and Millet, besides often asking after his old friends Emile Bernard and Gauguin. He would seem absolutely normal if it were not for certain confidential confessions such as 'There really is something or other

WALLED FIELD (SEEN FROM THE ASYLUM AT ST. RÉMY). 1889-1890.
NEUE STAATSGALERIE, MUNICH

out of order in my brain' and the confessions, too, made in his
paintings and drawings.

The first landscape which, it seems, he executed at St. Paul, in
early June, is also the first of his works in which a new sensibility
and style appear. The subject was the view from Vincent's window,
which therefore naturally occurs in many of his works at this time.
He describes the picture, *Mountain Landscape*, in the following
terms: 'In the foreground a cornfield, ravaged and flattened after a
storm. Then the wall enclosing it and beyond some grey-green
olive trees, huts and hills. Lastly, high up on the canvas, a big
white and grey cloud merging into blue sky.' The characteristic
hatching of the Arles period is here replaced by curvilinear, leaping,
turbulent brush strokes. The former short, straight lines, cut up

OLD MAN WEEPING. NOVEMBER 1882.
V. W. VAN GOGH COLLECTION, LAREN

into acute angles, have been prolonged to form serpentine sinuo-
sities, the unmistakable symptom, according to Dr. Peyron's
diagnosis, of epileptoid psychosis. Vincent had never previously
made a cloud so important. But the massive cloud in this picture

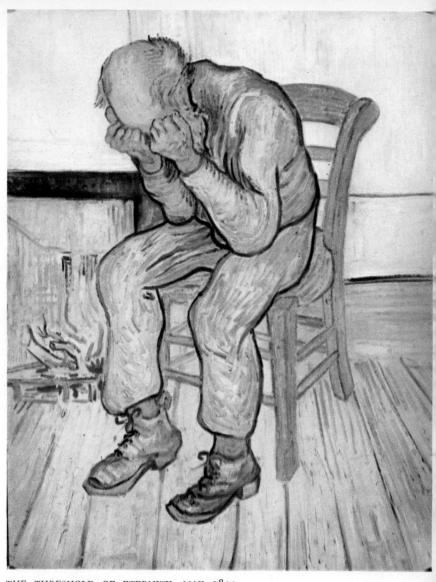

THE THRESHOLD OF ETERNITY. MAY 1890.
KRÖLLER-MÜLLER RIJKSMUSEUM, OTTERLO

squeezes out the sky, which the painter had formerly been fond of
extending, in a deep blue, across the background of his landscapes.
The contour of the foothills is rendered by a slightly undulating line
which was to become spasmodic, plunging and brusquely agitated

ROCKY GROUND. 1889-1890. PRIVATE COLLECTION

in a work of July 1889, *Hills at St. Rémy* (p. 169). The latter is a
chaotic landscape, with a colour scheme, unique among Vincent's
paintings, of dull greys, yellows, blues and greens, but an
amazingly impetuous design. In all these paintings, as also
in the drawings of this period, for example *Cypresses* (p. 210),
and still more in subsequent works, the irrefutable signs can
be identified of the psychotic disorder of which Vincent himself
confesses that he felt the effects both physically and mentally.
In *Starry Night* (p. 177), dating from June 1889, stars whirl
in a thickly painted sky, ploughed by heavy spirals which unroll
like monstrous, glistening caterpillars above the sleeping town.
Cornfield and Cypresses (Cat. 173), also painted in June, is a masterpiece in the artist's new style. There is great ease of invention in the
sinuous rhythm that governs the entire composition. The violet

mountains of the background have curling shapes that repeat the scroll formation of the clouds. The ochre cornfields, the green grass, the silvery olive-trees and the sombre cypresses are inflected with decorative undulations in the limpid air. *Cornfield with Reaper* (Cat. 171) also painted in June 1889, has the same subject as *Mountain Landscape,* the view from Vincent's window which he was to represent again and again at different hours of the day and on different days of the seasons. The five pictures of cypresses from June 1889 are also important. 'They are as beautiful in their lines and proportions as an Egyptian obelisk,' Vincent used to say. But actually his cypresses are more like huge bronze flames darting upwards either towards the tormented forms of clouds or into a nocturnal sky adorned with a crescent moon. 'I'm surprised', he writes, 'that they haven't yet been painted as I see them.' But it would be difficult for eyes which only studied appearances to see cypresses as Vincent did, with the eyes of his rapturous imagination. For at St. Rémy he had begun to invent a chimerical world very different from that he had erected at Arles, as a convinced realist, after nature. In his pictures of cypresses the trees, the clouds, the ground, the bushes and the hills all undulate, twine, swell and curve. The brush-strokes writhe in a tangle of glutinous paints. This style is especially evident in the *Two Women and Cypresses* (Cat. 176). But it can equally well be noted in the *Huts* and still more in the *Olive-Trees* (Cat. 177) where lines, planes and masses all join in a wild saraband.

There is passionate movement and a tumultuous rhythm in these paintings, quite distinct from the stately harmonies of the Arles compositions. Yet they are controlled by a correct estimation of plastic values and of their proportions and relations. Moreover, though they interpret extremely keen sensations, such values are coherently distributed in a uniform space. It is true that the line is often inflated, heavy and thick, construction sometimes weak and colour deprived of purity and brilliance, especially when mixed with zinc white, while the chrome no longer attains the 'high yellow note' which had intoxicated the artist in the previous year. He has lost his sense of the vertical and horizontal. He is attracted by asymmetrical and oblique form and the typical sinuous curve of baroque art. Yet he does not appear to be conscious of this tendency. Referring to his *Cornfield with Reaper,* he writes: 'I saw in the reaper—who was a vague figure toiling like a fiend in the heat of the day to finish his task—an image of death, with humanity as corn beneath the sickle ... but there was nothing gloomy about the affair. It was proceeding in full sunlight, under a shower of fine gold.' He takes pains to elucidate his meaning. 'It was an image of death ... but I was looking for something like a *half-smile* ... personally I find it rather curious to have seen such a thing through the iron bars of a prison-cell.' In other words the amenity, the peaceful beauty, the 'half-smile' that he wished to express, was betrayed by the recurrence of those impulses in him which arose burdened by all the confusion in the dark depths of his mind and submerged his more explicit purpose. The pressure of morbid tendencies and the periodical attacks of his malady were henceforth to drive further and further from his thoughts the cherished ideal of calm and serenity.

On the 6th July Dr. Peyron gave Vincent permission to visit Arles escorted by Trabu, the chief warder. He was warmly welcomed by the Ginoux family and remained for some hours with them. He also went to see Rachel, the prostitute to whom he had presented his severed ear. He packed up the few pictures he had not been able to take with him on the 3rd May. He returned to the asylum delighted with his day's excursion. But next morning, while he was painting the race-course preserved among the ruins of the ancient Roman city of Glanum, another fit seized him. He was carried back unconscious to the asylum. It was three weeks before he regained his reason. The fit was the most violent and the longest he had ever had. It left him trembling, stunned and frightened. He could not delude himself any longer. Other fits would be sure to follow. But he refused to let discouragement get the better of him and to resign himself to a purely vegetative existence. He determined to continue the struggle. For he had once declared: 'I can very well do without a benevolent deity in my life and also in my painting. But I can't do without something which is bigger than myself and constitutes my very life, the capacity to create.' So long as a breath of life remained to him, so long as he

IRISES. MAY 1890. V. W. VAN GOGH COLLECTION, LAREN

'*I'm working on a canvas of pinks over a bright green background and two others of big bunches of violet irises, one being set against a pink background, with a harmonious, mellow effect due to the combination of greens, pinks and violets. The other bunch, on the contrary, of violet shading into carmine and pure Prussian blue, is thrown into relief by a brilliant lemon-yellow background, other yellow tones appearing in the vase and the base on which it stands. Here the violently opposed complementaries are intensified in their effect by their very antagonism.*'
Letter to Theo

retained the least desire to create, he would carry on the battle. His weapon would be work, 'my best lightning-conductor'. By the beginning of September he was able to hold a brush again. As he was not allowed to paint out of doors he made a copy, from memory, of his *Bedroom at Arles* (p. 181), another of the *Pietà* of Delacroix (Cat. 181) and an angel's head after Rembrandt. He again painted the view from his window and retouched some recent studies. The grounds of the asylum provided him with a number of subjects, such as tree-trunks covered with ivy and moss among ferns (Cat. 178) and a stone bench. Whenever he was given permission to go out he engaged in a regular struggle to depict the twisted forms and grey foliage of the olive-trees. 'But they're very, very difficult', he wrote to Theo. He also remarked later, referring to his pictures of *Olive-Trees* (Cat. 179, 180): 'It suits and attracts me to work in the open air, which is all gold and silver.' Now that he had re-established relations with the world he was exploring afresh the inexhaustible variety of natural forms, his eagerness stimulated by the two months of enforced abstinence he had been obliged to undergo. The after-effects of his fit wore off and his strength returned. He himself notes: 'I am toiling like a man possessed. My rage for work is grimmer than ever.' In fact, over a period of three months, from September to November, he accumulated canvas after canvas, including landscapes, numerous copies of engravings by Millet (Cat. 182) and lastly portraits. Some of the latter were striking successes. Above all, *Portrait of the Chief Warder Trabu* (p. 189), who looked like an 'old Spanish noble', is a masterly work, subtle in colour and given a sharp impact by amazingly spirited drawing. Two *Self-portraits* are notable. One was painted in September 1889 shortly after the recent attack (p. 229). The other may be dated October-November. By that time his health had been temporarily restored. The face is calmer, with fewer signs of stress, and even seems to have filled out a little. This portrait, the last of himself that he left (p. 237), has an unaccustomed freshness of colouring in its blues and pale greens, reddish brown and light yellow. If it were not for the fierce eyes, which in all the self-portraits seem fixed upon some mysterious vision, beyond this world, the work could be taken to represent a

PATH THROUGH PINE TREES. 1890. V. W. VAN GOGH COLLECTION, LAREN

moment of relaxation and rehabilitation in the life of the painter.

But not all his work was so successful. The *Male Portrait* (Cat. 191), no doubt painted at the end of the year 1889, still has a certain dash and authority. But that of the *Schoolboy*, dated January 1890, shows some negligence, especially in the treatment of the hand and in articulation of volume (p. 205). It seems a mistake to refer the *Male Portrait* to the Arles period. The marked backward inclination of the figure, the extreme distortion of the nose and left cheek, the broken, zigzag lines in the face and the whole style of this work point to the St. Rémy development. Moreover, there is no reason to suppose the sitter to have been an actor. He was most probably merely one of Dr. Peyron's boarders.

During the autumn Vincent was chiefly inspired by trees, pines in the garden of the St. Paul asylum (Cat. 184), poplars on the hill (Cat. 185), the imposing bulk of mulberry-trees, a forest of pines in waning daylight (Cat. 186), twisted olive-trees ready for plucking

(Cat. 187), the big plane-trees of the St. Rémy boulevard or a trunk struck by lightning as in the *Hospital Grounds* (p. 185).

That winter he painted the *Ravine* (*Les Péroulets*) (Cat. 189), incidentally a copy of a picture on this subject executed in October, and the *Walled Field at Sunset* (Cat. 190), simply another version of the view from his window, together with some works of no importance. But apart from these productions he was wholly occupied in copying engravings by Millet, the *Siesta,* the *Return from the Fields,* the *Reaper* and lastly the *Sower.* The theme was one he had always had at heart. He returned to it constantly throughout his life, from the Borinage period to the end at Auvers. (See pp. 191-195.) Although in his copy of the *Sower* he followed the design fairly closely, he invented surprisingly fresh colour, thought the whole subject out again, made it his own and created an original work from it.

Dr. Peyron had warned him that another attack might be expected at Christmas. Vincent was by this time subject to hallucinations bearing on religion. He wrote to Theo: 'If I get into a state of religious exaltation again, then I shan't hesitate, I'd like to leave *at once*, without giving any reason. . . . *I mean this.*' Then realised the seriousness of the situation. Pissarro had recommended a certain Dr. Gachet of Auvers-sur-Oise, who liked artists and might be prepared to look after Vincent. Gachet immediately agreed to do so. At Christmas the expected attack occurred. But it was less acute and shorter than the patient had feared. A week later he was back at work again.

At the beginning of 1890 he made four versions of the *L'Arlésienne* (Madame Ginoux) after a drawing by Gauguin (Cat. 193). Rembrandt, Delacroix and Daumier also furnished him with opportunities for distraction and work. Lastly, in February, he painted *Prisoners at Exercise* (p. 209), after a woodcut by Gustave Doré. The captives tramping round in a circle guarded by uniformed warders, under towering walls, reminded Vincent of the distress of men like himself and his companions, who had lost their freedom. Nothing is more affecting than the endless rotation of these marching figures, their circular movement emphasised, in its monotony, by their radiating shadows.

PORTRAIT OF THE ARTIST WITH PALETTE. SEPTEMBER 1889.
COLLECTION OF MR. AND MRS. JOHN HAY WHITNEY, NEW YORK

'*It is said, and I can well believe it, that it is difficult to know oneself. But it isn't easy, either, to paint oneself. So I am working on two portraits of myself at this moment, since I have no other model and it is high time I paid a little attention to the face. One of the portraits was begun as soon as I got up. I was thin, and devilish pale.*

'*I used deep blue violet, making the head whitish, with yellow hair, so that a certain effect of colour is obtained. . . .*'
Letter to Theo

Spring returned. It was the third Vincent had spent in Provence. Through his barred window he could see grass and poppies growing in the enclosed field he had first painted in May 1889 and so often since. In April he painted it once more as *The Fenced Field* (p. 213), further accentuating the style of presentation begun in the *Mountain Landscape* and its variant *Cornfield with Reaper*. It was still the same field, with the same wall round it, the same distant houses and hills and the same perfectly circular sun. But now the whole scene was rendered without reference to reality. The painter, carried away by his passion for extremes, prolonged, weighted and distorted his forms to an unprecedented extent. The foreground, hatched yellow and green, rises and swells unduly in its rush towards the spectator, the wall bulging under its powerful pressure. The horizon is forced back to the top of the canvas, the massive rocks in the distance reel, the sky is so constricted that there is scarcely room in it for the sun.

After this date the artist's frenzy affects all he undertakes. The earth expands and cracks, mountains are convulsed, clouds whirl madly, stars gyrate like fireworks, trees writhe as if in rage, vegetation rolls forward like a breaking wave, distance overlaps foreground, clouds drop into trees and the ground leaps as though to assault the heavens. In this disjointed world of nature in delirium the rules of dimension, proportion and architecture explode under attacks of destructive violence. Perspective becomes fragmentary. Lines of sight fly in all directions. The brush strokes swing this way and that in furious curves or come to a sudden end. Colour is laid on in touches now broad, now threadlike. Examples are to be seen in *At the Foot of the Alpilles* (Cat. 194), *Field of Red Poppies* (Cat. 195) and *Road with Cypresses* (Cat. 197), the latter picture so well known and yet always a surprise to the observer. The moon and stars depicted seem to bore into the canvas like gimlets, the road wriggles away like a snake and the nearly black cypresses brandish their crests in a sky of milky blue. There is not a single vertical or horizontal, not even a straight line in the painting, apart from the yellowish brown diagonals of the field of corn. Undulating lines alone are drawn, all with a tendency to coil, twine or form circles.

THATCHED COTTAGE SURROUNDED BY CYPRESSES. 1890. V. W. VAN GOGH COLLECTION, LAREN

FIELD UNDER STORMY SKY. JULY 1890. V. W. VAN GOGH COLLECTION, LAREN

Gyration is one of van Gogh's most obsessive symbols. Previously its rhythm had represented the brilliance of stars and lamps and the arrangement of space behind certain of his portraits. In the works executed at St. Rémy it is extended to trees, rocks, clouds, gusts of wind, animate and inanimate objects. Brushstrokes, formerly so short, sharp and firm, are now elongated and produce arcs, while forms, instead of being carved out ruggedly in the mass, become rounded. The chaotic curves and counter-curves of *The Ravine* and the men marching in a circle in *Prisoners at Exercise* exemplify these tendencies. They are translations into pictorial language of a poetic and metaphysical idea summed up by the artist himself in the extraordinary phrase, 'Life is probably round'. He too, like his *Prisoners*, was tramping in a circle behind the bars of his cell, round and round incessantly, a permanent captive, walled up in his loneliness, held fast between walls like the field he could see from his window, like the stream at the bottom of the Ravin des Peroulets, the fir-tree in its forest, the thistle growing among the blackened ruins, the star hanging in the vault of heaven. Infinity and immensity haunted his dreams. His brush or pencil thrust back the bounds of space, probed the limits of the visible universe. 'Vast as the night and the light', Baudelaire had written in a famous poem. It was the vastness in both that continually obsessed van Gogh. In his work he only turned from the sun and its rays, which deliver mankind from the bonds of oppression and the moment, to replace sunlight by the moon, the stars and the infinity of night. He had already hung a star and a crescent moon in the background of the portrait of Lieutenant Milliet, and set the starry veil of night behind the painting of Eugène Boch. It was in night and stars, in the series of his *Starry Nights*, that he tried to dissipate or soothe his anguish. He was impelled by a similar aspiration, in May 1890, to paint the picture appropriately named *The Threshold of Eternity* (p. 221), depicting an old man seated in the chimney corner, his face mournfully buried in his hands. Vincent intended the figure 'to convey the feeling of an eternal fireside'.

He had drawn such a figure, an old man in almost the same attitude, seven years earlier, at The Hague (p. 220). At one time

HYACINTH STALKS. SPRING 1890. V. W. VAN GOGH COLLECTION, LAREN

his dreams had been of the future. But now, as if he really wished to abolish the barriers of time, he was turning back to memories of his childhood and youth. 'They come flooding in upon me', he noted. He began to talk in affectionate terms of his parents. He wrote a letter full of filial devotion to his aged mother on her birthday. He had already, in October 1888, painted a portrait of her from a photograph (Cat. 146). He now meant to paint some more pictures for her and his sister. He often thought of Holland, the places where he had lived and the people he had known. Forgetting his previous sarcastic remarks about the Amsterdam and Hague painters, he refers to them with surprising indulgence. 'I'm haunted by an intense longing to see my old friends and the northern countryside again,' he exclaimed on the 10th September 1889. When the winter came, the bare trees, the cold, the rain and the snow caused him to see Provence under the aspect of the great plains of the north. He noted, referring to the *Self-portrait* he had painted in September, 'Although I've lived for years in Paris, London and other great cities, I still look more or less like a Zundert peasant.'

He reached the point of wanting to leave the Midi. Much as he loved it, he felt somehow that he did not wish to die there. For his regression to thoughts of his childhood and native land, his new need of maternal affection, were fore-warnings of his approaching death. To close the cycle and return to the womb will always be man's last desire. 'Life' was indeed 'round'. Such retrograde tendencies can also be traced in his work. Just as he had copied, in the Borinage, Millet's *Field Labour,* he now copies it afresh at St. Rémy. And it is interesting to note that his reapers, sowers, diggers and weeders are represented in a style resembling that of Nuenen. His *Hovels* of April 1890 are 'a memory of the north' (Cat. 192). Neither in his letters nor in his pictures is there now any trace of the extraordinary exaltation into which he had once been thrown by colour. He makes no further reference to the 'high yellow note', or to the Japanese masters. In 1888 he had gone into ecstasies over the awe-inspiring reds and greens of the *Boat of Christ*. But it was now another picture by Delacroix, the *Odalisques* at Montpellier, which interested him, owing to its muted tints and

PORTRAIT OF THE ARTIST. NOVEMBER 1889. MUSÉE DE L'IMPRESSIONNISME, PARIS

gradations. His own colour no longer exhibited the boldness, purity and intensity which had startled the Parisians in 1888. In the *Hospital Grounds at St. Rémy* (p. 185), *The Threshold of Eternity* (p. 221), the blues have grown pale, the yellows too light in tint, and the reds are subdued. Again, the *Irises* and *White Roses* (Cat. 198) of May 1890, though very pleasingly painted canvases, are far from rivalling the *Sunflowers*. The intensely blue skies of the *Pont de l'Anglois*, the *Market Gardens* and *Vincent's House* have disappeared. His skies are now overloaded with vermicular, trailing forms of unpleasant aspect, when they are not obliterated by great clouds as heavy with storm as his own spirit. If he does employ a greater variety and vivacity of colour, no matter how aggressive, discordant and virulent he makes it, the picture still doesn't 'come off'. Both harmony and the light of nature are absent.

The admirable coherence and majesty of the Arles period are gone. Thereafter his work becomes as uncertain as his temper, with alternations of resignation and anxiety, doubt and hope, excellence and mediocrity. He was himself well enough aware of it. In notifying Theo of the despatch of a roll of canvases, he writes: 'In this lot there is nothing much any good except the cornfield, the mountain, the orchard, the olive-trees with the blue hills, the portrait and the racecourse starting-point. The rest looks *insignificant* to me, because the personal touch, lines that are felt, are lacking.' Something had really given way in him, not wholly on account of his malady. Or rather his illness does not seem to have been due to a lesion of the brain, but to some much more remote cause. His life had been one of noble ambition defrauded, plans that came to nothing, defeat after defeat and moral constraint. He was keeping up the struggle. But he had lost his faith. He wondered why he should 'continue to paint, as it's such an effort and one gets nothing out of it . . . I think it's crazy.' Yet that madness helped him to endure the *other* and also to retain his dignity. For he never forgot for a moment what he owed his brother, which he could only repay by work. And now Theo had recently married and his wife was expecting a child. Vincent realised what a burden he was going to be, as a sick, sullen and embittered failure, on his brother's new domesticity. The humiliation and remorse were worse than his fits of morbid depression and the sufferings that followed each of his attacks. He was haunted, moreover, by 'excruciating religious ideas'. The hallucinations of the mentally afflicted do in fact often assume a mystical character. Vincent proceeded to paint a *Good Samaritan* after Delacroix and a

Resurrection of Lazarus (Cat. 196) after an etching by Rembrandt. They are works of little interest. His successes were in fact now rare. Touching as the paintings of this period are, there is less magic in them than singularity, more putrefaction than excitement and less originality than oddity. Through this baroque style the artist, feeling himself excluded from the universe and despairing of his return to it, takes the only course open to him by creating an artificial, substitute universe. He is thus driven to disorder, immoderation, the exasperation of movement and caricatural expression. Van Gogh's malady was stylistic.

His last works, in spite of brilliant exceptions, the last flares of his genius, cannot be put on the same level as that of his Arlesian period, when he saw nothing but light, cohesion and wisdom in the world and the thanksgiving song of the universe was bursting from his heart. His final paintings imply discontinuity, dispersal and disorganisation. They are dogged by impotence and at the same time in revolt against it. Yet in spite of this conflict, or because of it, they sometimes rise to sublimity. Formerly he had translated his ideal of health and serenity into static, balanced shapes, strictly modulated and organised, which represented solid, unshakable stability. But now he had turned to depict pain, love and death. He lent his own sensations and torments to natural phenomena. Referring to his drawing of the great pine in the asylum grounds, he notes the 'proud, unchangeable character' of that 'sombre giant, arrogant in defeat'. He describes elsewhere 'the combination of red ochre, green saddened by grey and black outlines defining contour, which carries a suggestion of the anguish from which my companions in misfortune often suffer. It's called *black-red*.' Again, he mentions the 'pale smile of a last rose', 'parched and melancholy lands' and the 'sickly, greenish-pink smile of the last flower of autumn'.

In the poetic phrasing of the 'correspondences' indicated by these quotations we can discern extreme sensitivity, infinite disenchantment and incurable melancholy. It is that of a man who expects nothing more from life or from himself. He resembles the great tree 'struck by lightning' to which he alludes in one of his letters to Emile Bernard. The external world is forever presenting him with some symbol of his wretched and disordered existence. Yet he does not let himself drift. For the time being at least he continues on his way, though he knows it leads nowhere. 'I have no longer the slightest wish to succeed. I only paint in order to withdraw from life.' Nevertheless, certain happy events were about to introduce a little light into his sombre, secluded existence. On the 1st February 1890 Theo informed him of the birth of a son, to be christened Vincent-Willem after the artist himself, who was delighted to hear the news. Soon afterwards he had the satisfaction of reading a long article by Albert Aurier, the Parisian critic, enthusiastically praising his painting. Satisfaction is perhaps too strong a word, for in his letter of thanks to Aurier he will not accept the latter's compliments, referring him to Monticelli, 'to whom I owe so much' and to Gauguin, who is a 'greater colourist than myself'. Nor was this false modesty in a man of Vincent's generous temper. On the 14th February 1890 he learned that his *Red Vines* had been bought for four hundred francs by Anna Boch, sister of the Belgian painter whose portrait he had executed at Arles. So he had begun to succeed at last. But it does not seem that he took any pleasure in the fact. In any case, six days later he was struck down by so violent and painful an attack that he did not recover until the end of April. This time he appealed to his brother, who decided to withdraw him from the asylum. He was to leave for Auvers-sur-Oise very soon. Meanwhile, he resumed work.

The St. Rémy paintings having been already examined, we may add a few words about the drawings done there. They also deal with most of the subjects treated in the paintings, such as the hospital grounds, the field of corn, the Alpilles, the cypresses and the sower. The same sinuous, writhing line and the same turbulence of composition are evident. But in certain of the drawings, notably in his studies of the grounds and garden and for the *Hospital Fountain* (p. 203), the artist's hand grows steadier, achieving the draughtsmanship of the best period. Short parallel lines, dots, bristles, dashes, firm contours and impressive volumes return. Some drawings, such as *Cypresses by Moonlight* (p. 176), *The Walled Field* (p. 219), *Hyacinth Stalks* (p. 235), *Arum Lilies* (p. 242) and *Flowering Stalk* are actually prodigies of deep feeling, simplicity,

CHURCH AT AUVERS. 4-8 JUNE 1890. MUSÉE DE L'IMPRESSIONNISME, PARIS

ARUM LILIES. SPRING 1890. V. W. VAN GOGH COLLECTION, LAREN

confidence and dexterity. Here the draughtsman retains his mastery, though the painter may get lost among his colours.

Vincent looked forward with relief to his approaching departure. But he could not overcome his lassitude. In writing to inform Theo that he was sending him his latest canvases, including the *Cypresses,* a gift to Albert Aurier, he adds the request: 'Please beg M. Aurier not to write any more articles on my painting. Try to make him understand that he is mistaken about me, for I really feel too exhausted by my misfortunes to stand publicity. It distracts me to paint. But to hear others discuss my paintings is more painful to me than he realises.' The confession is deeply significant. He already knew for certain that he was to leave the St. Paul hospital, would no longer have to mingle with lunatics and be worried by nuns. He knew that he would soon be free at last. But no prospect now seemed to please, stimulate or even interest him. He had already ceased to be of this world.

ON the 16th May 1890 he left for Tarascon to take the train to Paris. When Theo introduced him, next day, to his young wife, Jo, she was quite surprised to see a man of robust appearance, sound mind and, whatever might be the matter with him, 'stronger than Theo'. She was perfectly right, incidentally, for her husband's health was worse than that of her brother-in-law. For a few days Vincent forgot his troubles in the company of Theo, Jo and the baby. But he soon had to leave the comfort and peace of their hospitable domesticity. On the 21st May, a fine spring day, he arrived at Auvers-sur-Oise and called upon Dr. Paul-Ferdinand Gachet. The doctor was an extremely cultivated man, interested in everything, especially painting. He painted and engraved himself in his leisure hours and enjoyed the company of artists, particularly the impressionists. He had a highly original mind, receptive of all the new ideas of the day. He welcomed his new patient frankly and sympathetically, escorting him to the St. Aubin, an inn which Vincent was to leave three days later for less expensive accommodation in a café managed by Gustave Ravoux in the main square near the town hall.

As soon as Vincent had moved in he set off to inspect the neighbourhood. He was so pleased with it that he immediately began, with enthusiasm, to paint some old thatched cottages, which reminded him of Brabant, as well as two studies of chestnut-trees in flower (Cat. 199). He visited Dr. Gachet regularly, dining with him once a week. The two men had rapidly become friends. They had similar temperaments and ideas. The doctor, moreover, on examining Vincent's works, had seen signs of genius in them. On the 14th June after the artist had finished a portrait of Gachet in two sittings (Cat. 205), the latter declared himself, says the painter, 'an absolute *fanatic*' about it. The subject is represented against a cobalt blue background. He wears a white cap and a Prussian blue jacket. The right elbow rests on a red table, the right hand holding a branch of digitalis, an allusion to the doctor's special field of heart disease. At Gachet's request Vincent made a copy, much better than the original, of this portrait. The copy is an authentic masterpiece (p. 252), despite its sinuous lines, some artificial variation in the drawing and a mannered style. On the other hand the portraits of Mademoiselle Gachet, Mademoiselle Ravoux (Cat. 210) and *The Man with the Cornflower* (Cat. 206) are weak. Some sixty other pictures were painted by van Gogh during his two months at Auvers. Of these that of the town hall (Cat. 215) and the church (p. 241), though the buildings are made to look very unsafe, exercise an irresistible fascination. The village and its surroundings (Cat. 216), with steep, narrow lanes (Cat. 202) and houses half buried in their gardens, the cottages at Cordeville (p. 245), the banks of the Oise and the garden of Daubigny's house [the French landscape painter Charles François Daubigny, 1817-78] were often the

STREET IN AUVERS. JUNE 1890. ATHENAEUM MUSEUM, HELSINKI

THATCHED COTTAGES AT CORDEVILLE. ABOUT 10 JUNE 1890. MUSÉE DE
L'IMPRESSIONNISME, PARIS

scene of paintings made on the spot by van Gogh in characteris-
tically swift brush-strokes. But many shortcomings can now be
detected in these pictures. The great plains surrounding Auvers
made a special appeal to him, perhaps because they reminded him
of his youth. He wrote to his mother: 'I am completely engrossed
by these huge plains of standing corn, backed by hills. They are
vast as the sea, very delicate yellow, very pale green and very soft
mauve. Part of the land is under cultivation, dotted with flowering
potato-plants. The sky is blue, with white, pink and violet tints.
I feel utterly at peace, almost too much so. I believe I'm capable
of painting the scene.'

The *Plain, Auvers* (p. 217), the *The Road near Auvers* (Cat. 207) and some other paintings on this theme could not be better described. He could observe the subject and define it in the right words. But the landscapes he painted while feeling so peaceful and calm as he contemplated such peaceful and calm horizons are disturbing. The lines are restless, the impasto has a violent quality, the brush-strokes flounder. Yet these are the least tormented visions that Vincent had of this glorious summer, the last of his life. It is hard to understand, too, why he should have imparted such agitation to the pure and simple architecture of the little Gothic church of Auvers and streaked it with such explosive colour. Why, again, did he impose the distracted rhythm of the St. Rémy cypresses on the trees in Daubigny's and Gachet's gardens? What were such unseasonable divagations and baroque excesses doing in the mellow and serene region of the Ile de France?

Theo, his wife and son, came to spend Sunday, the 8th June, with Vincent. He showed them, with childish delight, the local beauty spots. The visit cheered him up greatly. During the follow-

SHEAVES. JULY 1890. V. W. VAN GOGH COLLECTION, LAREN

PÈRE ÉLOI'S FARM AT AUVERS. 1890. MUSÉE DE L'IMPRESSIONISME, PARIS

ing days he painted canvas after canvas, working 'hard and fast'. He had made a few friends, in addition to the Gachet and Ravoux families, among the painters who came to seek inspiration at Auvers and the local inhabitants. He also came to know Gaston and René Secretan, two young students on vacation in the Oise country, who were often accompanied by their far from shy girl-friends. He was leading a regular life, hardly drinking at all and eating well. But uneasiness still beset him, as he confessed to Theo, without dwelling on the fact, for he knew how it would upset his brother. The latter had, moreover, grown very weak lately, while his wife's health and that of the child were also frail. Vincent accordingly allowed Theo to believe in the possibility of a cure, this belief being also encouraged by Dr. Gachet. It is not clear

CORNFIELD WITH CROWS. JULY 1890. V. W. VAN GOGH COLLECTION, LAREN

DR. GACHET'S HOUSE AT AUVERS. 1890.
V. W. VAN GOGH COLLECTION, LAREN

why the doctor could have entertained this illusion. But Vincent, with his usual penetration, observes: 'He is more sick than I am, or just about in the same condition.'

Meanwhile, van Gogh, with his mutilated ear, his eccentric behaviour, his casual labourer's clothing, his crumpled felt hat and the basket in which he carried his painting materials, seemed a scarecrow to the local people. Just as at Arles, the little boys ran after him. They, too, are said to have called him 'the madman'. René Secretan gives the following description of him: 'He was a queer fellow, of uncertain temper, cheerful one day and looking like an undertaker's man the next. Talkative enough with his nose in a glass, he would also spend whole hours in dumb contemplation or meditation.' The brothers Secretan and their set of high-spirited youngsters and obliging damsels enjoyed teasing Vincent. As a rule he put up with their chaff coolly enough. All the same, he suffered greatly from the amorous provocation to which he was subjected by the girls, who were hardly of a retiring disposition. René Secretan told a contributor to the periodical *Aesculape* that though van Gogh may have been timid with the young ladies he showed signs of sexual perversion, as is often the case with epileptics. The same witness explained further, in reply to Dr. Doiteau: 'You've found exactly the right word; *depressed*, perhaps *tormented* and most certainly *afflicted*.'

It is difficult to believe that the peculiarities of conduct so clearly evident to a very young man had escaped the notice of the shrewd Dr. Gachet, all the more so since the relations between doctor and patient had soon taken a turn for the worse, owing to the frequency of arguments which annoyed Gachet and dangerously weakened van Gogh. In any case Vincent gradually began to lose confidence in his medical adviser. He found that however obstinately he worked his strength was leaving him. That he was well aware of his condition is clear from a letter he wrote to Theo, found in his pocket after his death. 'Well, that work of mine is endangering my life. My reason has half foundered under it.' At the same time he felt that he was losing his faculties of expression. His style was getting slack, his line hardening, his touch going astray and his colour dimming. Clumsily sketched forms, dissonant tones,

PORTRAIT OF DR. GACHET. JUNE 1890. MUSÉE DE L'IMPRESSIONNISME, PARIS

smeared paint, irresolute composition and a dry, mechanical, devitalised handling all attested irremediable decline. The portrait of *Mademoiselle Gachet at the Piano* (Cat. 211) looks decidedly sentimental in comparison with *L'Arlésienne against Pink Background* or *Le Mousmé*. The *Auvers Town Hall* of July 1890 is loosely drawn and poorly coloured when contrasted with the energetic construction and glowing hues of *Vincent's House,* painted in September 1888. Again, one of the best pictures of June 1890, the *Auvers Plain,* is much inferior to the *Crau Market-gardens,* a similar subject treated at Arles two years earlier. The latter is distinguished by the tranquillity of its long horizontals, the density of its atmosphere, the utter fixity of objects and their rigorous disposition, the sumptuous quality and depth of its yellows, reds, greens and blues perfectly attuned to wonderfully assured drawing. But in the former the lines shake, the paint is too fluid, the colour lacks vigour and the brush-strokes precision. We are no longer confronted by a vast plain expanding in the sunlight and loaded with harvests to come, but by a panorama evoked from desultory dreaming, by no means colourless, and yet lightless. It is a plain which the rays of the summer sun have failed to warm. In spite of the labours of the brush it remains as cold as porcelain.

Vincent continued to accumulate canvases, polishing off at least one a day, and to draw. Dr. Gachet had taught him etching. He copied in that medium the portrait he had painted of the doctor. But there was no future for him there, for the end was approaching. On Sunday, the 6th July, he went to Paris. Jo was convalescent from an illness. The child was not well. Theo was greatly worried over a dispute, just then at its most acrimonious, with his employers Boussod and Valadon. Such was the situation when the two brothers met. It is not known what passed at their interview. Vincent's susceptibilities may have been wounded by some hasty words. He may himself have realised that the expense of supporting him was becoming more than a family so afflicted with ill-health and money troubles could bear. He may have believed, in short, that he was usurping the place of a child that was only just being kept alive. At any rate, he returned to Auvers in great distress and wrote a letter to his brother and sister-in-law couched in excep-

tionally serious terms. 'My impression is that as we are all some-
what bewildered and preoccupied by our affairs there is not much
point in insisting upon a very clear definition of the position in
which we find ourselves. I was rather surprised by what I thought
was your attempt to bring matters to a head. How can I do anything about it? Can I do anything whatever to meet your wishes?'
It was Jo who answered, doing her best to reassure him, and at
the same time telling him they were leaving for Holland. His reply
was pathetic. 'I was rather afraid—not much, but a little—that you
were beginning to be alarmed at having to keep me. But Jo's
letter shows clearly that you are well aware that I am just as
worried over it as you are. As soon as I got back here I started
work again, though I could hardly hold the brush. But I knew
quite well what I wanted and I've painted another three big
canvases.'

No doubt he did know what he wanted. But did he yet know
whether he could do it? He goes on: 'The subject is a great
expanse of cornland under overcast skies and I did not need to
go out of my way to express its melancholy and utter loneliness.'
One of the three big canvases he mentions is undoubtedly *Field
under Stormy Sky* (p. 233). The sky certainly is stormy, sombre and
heavy, darkened by packed clouds. A pale light falls from it,
investing the earth with a cadaverous green. The picture is a
mournful one, full of tragic presentiment. Vincent himself felt as
sombre and oppressed as his funereal sky. He had become extremely
irritable. During one of his last visits to Dr. Gachet he flew into a
rage over a trifle, accusing his host of leaving a canvas by Guillaumin unframed. When his attitude grew too aggressive, the doctor
turned a stern look upon him and his anger immediately evaporated.

On the 23rd July he wrote to Theo: 'There was a lot I wanted to
tell you. But then the mood passed and anyhow I feel it would be
useless.' Had he meant to confess that he would never climb the
heights again, that he was finished and all was lost? Most probably.
For there would really be no point in uttering complaints that
would make no difference whatever to his fate. That would be an
utter waste of time. And yet he started another picture, *Cornfield*

PATH ACROSS FIELDS. 1890. V. W. VAN GOGH COLLECTION, LAREN

with Crows (p. 249). A great poet, also on the threshold of madness, had attached a poignant significance to such birds, expressed in the 'Nevermore!' of Poe's *The Raven*. In Vincent's painting crows fly across corn tinged with red towards a lowering sky, inscribing it with omens of coming disaster. On the 27th July, in fact, the last act of the tragedy was played out.

It was a Sunday, as it had been a Sunday when he severed his ear. The village was almost empty. He left Ravoux' place and walked towards the hamlet of Chaponval. In the rue Boucher he entered a farmyard, concealed himself behind a manure heap and fired a revolver bullet into his groin. Then, with his hand pressed to the bleeding wound, he returned to the Ravoux café, climbed the stairs to his attic and collapsed like an injured animal. Shortly afterwards Ravoux found him at the point of death, and sent at once for the local doctor. Gachet and his son arrived at the inn that evening. The version here given of van Gogh's suicide has been deliberately altered from that usually accepted, which is based on doubtful evidence. In that account Vincent is supposed to have ended his life 'in the fields', no further details being stated. But the testimony of M. Tralbaut contributed to the issue of *Aesculape* for December 1957 seems both more reliable and more likely. It has therefore been confidently adopted in the present text.

Van Gogh, then, was lying on his bed mortally wounded. At that period extraction of the bullet was impracticable. Nothing could be done but to notify Theo. The latter arrived at Auvers the next morning and spent the day at the dying man's bedside. Vincent was quite conscious. 'Don't weep,' he said. 'What I have done was best for all of us.' His brother tried to console him. But he answered: 'No use. I shall never be rid of this depression.' He died peacefully, without a word of complaint, on the 29th July 1890, at half-past one in the morning, aged thirty-seven years and four months.

On the 30th some of Vincent's friends, Tanguy, Emile Bernard, Laval, and André Bonger, Jo's brother, arrived from Paris for the funeral. He was buried in the little cemetery at Auvers, surrounded by fields of corn. Theo wrote to his aged mother: 'It is impossible to describe his sadness and find consolation. I shall be crushed by my grief for a long time. I shall never forget it. All one can say is that he has now found the rest he longed for. . . . Life was too great a burden for him. Yet, as so often happens, everyone now warmly praises his talent. O mother, we were so much alike!'

The similarity between the two brothers was soon to unite them in death. Two months later Theo's chronic nephritis took an acute form and his mind suddenly gave way. He was found dangerous to his family and confined, on the 14th October, in a private hospital directed by Dr. Blanche. Eventually his wife took him to Holland and he died there on the 25th January 1891. Twenty-three years later Jo had his remains transferred to Auvers-sur-Oise and interred beside his brother's. It was only there, united forever in their twin graves, that Vincent and Theo at last found the rest which had been denied them in life.

CHRONOLOGICAL LIST
OF PRINCIPAL WORKS

1. The Forge. June 1881.

2. Pastor Theodorus van Gogh.
June-July 1881.

3. The Sower. September 1881.

4. Windmills near Dordrecht. Aug. 1881.

5. Gate-Keeper's House. 1881.

6. Man by the Fire. November 1881.

7. Still Life with Jug. December 1881.

8. View of Scheveningen. January 1882.

9. Behind the Schenkweg. May 1882.

10. The Coast near Scheveningen.
August 1882.

11. Miners' Wives carrying Coal.
November 1882.

12. Girl with a Shawl. Jan.-Feb. 1883.

13. Woman Praying. March-April 1883.

14. Fisherman's Wife. August 1883.

15. Peasant at Work. September 1883.

16. Thatched Cottages. October 1883.

17. The Weaver. January 1884.

18. Woman Spinning. May 1884.

19. The Loom. May 1884.

20. The Weaver. May 1884.

21. Bullock Cart. July 1884.

22. Snow Scene. Aug.-Sept. 1884.

23. Lane near Nuenen. Oct. 1884-1886.

24. Street in Eindhoven. 1884.

25. Still Life with Stone Bottles.
November 1884.

26. Head of a Peasant smoking a Pipe.
November 1884.

27. Still Life with Mortar. Nov. 1884.

28. Peasants at Table. March 1885.   29. Head of a Peasant Girl. 1885.   30. Peasant Woman Sweeping.
March 1885.

31. Peasant Woman in a Red Bonnet.   32. Head of a Peasant Woman. May 1885.   33. Peasant Woman in a Brown Bonnet.
April 1885.   April-May 1885

34. Sunset. April 1885.   35. Cottage at Nightfall. May 1885.

36. The Potato Eaters. April 1885.

37. Head of a Brabant Peasant Woman. June 1885.

38. Still Life with Potatoes. Sept. 1885.

39. Work in the Fields. 1885.

40. Peasant Woman cashing Linen. 1885.

41. Still Life with Apples and Two Gourds. Sept.-Oct. 1885.

42. Still Life with Open Bible. Oct. 1885.

43. The Presbytery at Nuenen
October-November 1885.

44. Autumn Landscape with Four Trees.
November 1885.

45. Lane in Autumn. Oct.-Nov. 1885.

46. Self-Portrait. December 1885.

47. Working Girl. December 1885.

PARIS

48. La Guingette. 1886.

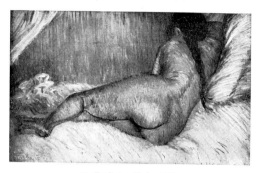

49. Reclining Nude. 1886.

. Montmartre The Street Lamps. 1886.

51. The Plaster Statuette. 1886.

52. The Moulin de la Galette. 1886.

53. The Moulin de la Galette. 1886.

54. Montmartre. 1886.

56. Fritillaries in a Copper Vase.
Summer 1886.

55. Red Gladioli. Summer 1886.

57. Hollyhocks. Summer 1886.

58. Roses and Sunflowers. Summer 1886.

59. The Boots. 1886-1887.

60. The Terrace of the Tuileries. 1886.

61. The Bois de Boulogne. 1886.

62. Portrait of Alexander Reid.
1886-1887.

63. Absinth. 1887.

64. Portrait of Père Tanguy. Jan. 1887.

65. Boulevard de Clichy. 1887.

66. View from Van Gogh's Room, Rue Lepic. 1887.

67. Still Life with Statuette. Spring 1887.

68. The Yellow Books (Parisian Novels). Spring 1887

69. Self-Portrait. 1887.

70. Self-Portrait. 1886-1887.

71. Self-Portrait. 1887.

72. Self-Portrait. 1887.

73. Self-Portrait. 1887.

74. Self-Portrait. 1887.

75. Self-Portrait in a Grey Hat. 1887

76. Self-Portrait. 1887.

77. Fishing in the Spring. 1887.

78. Woman by a Cradle. Spring 1887.

79. Restaurant Interior. Spring or Summer 1887.

80. Brush-Wood. 1887.

81. River Bank in the Spring. Spring 1887.

82. The Restaurant de la Sirène. Summer 1887.

83. Gardens on the Butte Montmartre. 1887.

84. The Banks of the Seine. Summer 1887.

85. The Pont de Chatou. Summer 1887.

87. Still Life with Carafe and Lemons. 1887.

86. The Pont d'Asnières. 1887.

88. Bastille Day (14 July) in Paris. 1887.

89. Factories at Clichy. 1887.

90. Factory Yard. 1887.

91. Italian Woman (La Segatori?).
Autumn 1887.

92. Portrait of Père Tanguy. 1887.

93. The Woman at Le Tambourin.
1887-1888.

95. Basket of Apples (« à l'ami Pissarro »).
1887

4. Japonaiserie: The Actor (after Kesai
Yeisen). Early 1888.

96. Japonaiserie: The Bridge (after
Hiroshige). Early 1888.

97. Self-Portrait at the Easel.
January-February 1888.

98. Snow at Arles. February 1888.

99. Sprig of Almond Blossom. February 1888.

100. The Viaduct at Arles. March 1888.

101. The Pont de Gleize, near Arles. March 1888.

102. The Pont de l'Anglois. March 1888.

103. Pear-Tree in Blossom. April 1888.

104. Tree in Blossom. April 1888.

105. Orchard. April 1888.

106. Orchard in Blossom with Cypresses. April 1888.

107. Van Gogh's House at Arles. May 1888.

108. Still Life with Majolica Jug.
May 1888.

109. Potatoes in a Yellow Dish.
Spring 1888.

110. View of Les Saintes-Maries.
June 1888.

111. The Sea at Les Saintes-Maries.
June 1888.

112. Whitewashed Cottages at Les
Saintes-Maries. June 1888.

113. Provençal Cottages. June 1888.

114 Field of Corn. June 1888.

115. Haystacks. June 1888.

116. Haystacks in Provence. June 1888.

117. La Crau : Market-Gardens. June 1888.

118. The Sower. June 1888.

119. The Zouave. June 1888.

120. Washerwomen. June 1888.

121. The Zouave. June-August 1888.

122. Haystacks. 1888.

123. Field with Corn Sheaves. 1888.

124. Haystacks in Wet Weather. Summer 1888.

125. La Maison de la Crau. 1888.

126. Thistles. August 1888.

127. The Painter on the Road
to Tarascon. August 1888.

128. Portrait of a Girl on a Rose Ground.
1888.

129. Garden by a House. 1888.

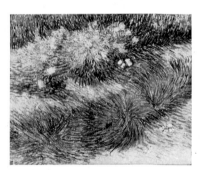

130. Oleanders. August 1888.

131. Corner of a Garden with Butterflies.
August 1888.

133. Sunflowers. August 1888.

132. Old Provençal Peasant (Patience Escalier).
August 1888.

134. Portrait of the Postman Roulin.
August 1888.

135. Caravans. August 1888.

136. Van Gogh's House at Arles
(The Yellow House). September 1888.

137. Restaurant at Arles. September 1888.

138. The All Night Café. September 1888.

139. Self-Portrait. Sept.-Nov. 1888.

140. Café Terrace at Night
(Place du Forum). September 1888.

141. The Belgian Painter Boch. Sept. 1888.

142. Starry Night on the Rhône.
September 1888.

143. The Tarascon Stage-Coaches.
September-October 1888.

144. Van Gogh's Room. October 1888.

145. Park at Arles. October 1888.

147. The Sower. October 1888.

146. The Artist's Mother (after a photo).
October 1888.

148. The Tree. October 1888.

149. The Pont de Trinquetaille. Oct. 1888.

150. Vineyard (The Green Vine). October 1888.

151. Les Alyscamps in Autumn.
November 1888.

152. Promenade at Arles (Memories of the
Garden at Etten). November 1888.

153. L'Arlésienne (Mme Ginoux).
November 1888.

154. Mme Roulin and her Baby.
November 1888.

155. Portrait of Armand Roulin.
November 1888.

156. Portrait of Armand Roulin.
November 1888.

157. Gaugin's Arm-Chair. December 1888.

158. Self-Portrait (« à l'ami Laval »).
November-December 1888.

159. The Hospital at Arles. Early 1889.

160. La Berceuse (Mme Roulin).
December 1888 - March 1889.

161. Still Life with Drawing-Board and
Onions. January 1889.

162. Still Life with Fruit-Basket and
Gloves. January 1889.

163. Portrait of Dr Rey. January 1889.

164. Vase of Poppies. 1889.

165. The Postman Roulin. Feb.-March 1889.

166. La Crau: Peach Trees in Blossom. March-April 1889.

167. View of Arles. April 1889.

168. The Garden of the Hospital at Arles.
April-May 1889.

169. The Old Willows. May 1889.

170. Irises. May 1889.

171. Corn Field with Reaper. June 1889.

172. Ripening Corn. 1889.

173. Corn Field and Cypresses. June 1889.

174. The Garden of the Asylum at St-Rémy. May-June 1889.

175. Corridor in the Asylum at St-Rémy. June 1889.

176. Two Women and Cypresses. June 1889 - February 1890.

177. Olive-Trees. June-July 1889.

178. Brush-Wood. September 1889.

179. Field of Olive-Trees. Sept.-Oct. 1889.

180. Field of Olive-Trees with Mauve Earth.
September-October 1889.

181. Pietà (after Delacroix). Sept. 1889.

182. The Reaper (after Millet).
September-November 1889.

183. The Evening Stroll. October 1889.

184. The Asylum at St-Rémy. Oct. 1889.

185. The Poplars on the Hill. Oct. 1889.

186. Pine-Trees at Sunset. Nov. 1889.

187. Olive Pickers. November 1889.

188. The Roadmenders. November 1889.

189. The Ravine (Les Péroulets).
December 1889.

190. Walled Field at Sunset
Winter 1889-1890.

191. Male Portrait. Winter 1889-1890.

192. Hovels (Memories of the North)
April 1890.

193. L'Arlésienne (after Gauguin).
January-February 1890.

194. At the Foot of the Alpilles.
April-May 1890.

195. Field of Red Poppies.
April-May 1890.

196. Resurrection of Lazarus
(after Rembrandt). May 1890.

197. Road with Cypresses. May 1890.

198. White Roses. May 1890.

199. Chestnut-Tree in Blossom. May 1890.

200. Mlle Gachet in the Garden.
1 June 1890.

201. Dr Gachet's Garden. 27 May 189

202. The Steps at Auvers. June 1890.

203. Wooded Landscape. 1890.

204. Roses and Anemones. June 1890.

205. Portrait of Dr Gachet.
About 4 June 1890.

206. The Man with the Cornflower.
June 1890.

207. The Road near Auvers. June 1890.

208. The Thicket. 1890.

210. Portrait of Mlle Ravoux. June 1890.

209. Girl Standing. June 1890.

211. Mlle Gachet at the Piano.
28-29 June 1890.

212. Landscape near Auvers. June 1890.

213. The Château d'Auvers. June 1890.

214. Les Vessenots at Auvers. July 1890.

215. The Town Hall at Auvers on Bastille Day. July 1890

216. View of Auvers. July 1890.

217. Sandstone Cottages at Chaponval.
July 1890.

218. The Plain near Auvers. July 1890.

219 The Plain at Auvers. July 1890.

BIBLIOGRAPHY

LA FAILLE (J.-B. de): *L'œuvre de Vincent van Gogh. Catalogue raisonné,* 4 volumes, Editions van Oest, Paris and Brussels 1928. In spite of a certain number of errors, inevitable in a work of this size, this Catalogue is still absolutely essential. The four volumes are laid out as follows:

I—*Painting: Catalogue.* The numbers run up to 824.
II—*Painting: Plates.* 857 works reproduced.
III—*Drawings, water-colours, lithographs, etchings: the Catalogue.* The numbers run up to 860.
IV—*Drawings: Plates.* 869 works reproduced.

LA FAILLE (J.-B. de): *Vincent van Gogh.* Preface by Charles Terrasse. Editions Hypérion, Paris 1939. A completely new edition with some important modifications to volumes I and II of the previous Catalogue. 833 pictures are reproduced, of which 16 are in colour.

LA FAILLE (J.-B. de): *Les faux van Gogh avec 176 reproductions.* Editions van Oest, Paris et Bruxelles 1930.

SCHERJON. DE GRUYTER: *Vincent van Gogh's great period: Arles, Saint-Rémy, Auvers-sur-Oise.* Complete Catalogue with 421 plates. Editions De Spieghel, Amsterdam 1937.

VAN BESELAERE (Walter): *De Hollandsche Periode (1880-1885) in het Werk van Vincent van Gogh.* 51 illustrations, with a preface by A. Vermeylen. Wereldbibliotheek, Amsterdam 1937.

HAMMACHER (A. M.): *Rijksmuseum Kröller-Müller: Catalogus van 270 Werken van Vincent van Gogh.* 16 reproductions in colour, 27 in black and white. Otterlo 1953 (first edition 1949).

TRALBAUT (Dr. Mark Edo): *Vincent van Gogh, in zijn Antwerpsche Periode.* Prefaced by some letters of V. W. van Gogh and W. van Beselaere. 57 illustrations in black and white, 4 plates in colour. Strengholt, Amsterdam 1948.

Apart from these essential works, some Exhibition Catalogues should be mentioned, since a certain number are indispensable for serious research:

LA FAILLE (J.-B. de): *L'époque française de van Gogh.* 43 plates. Bernheim Jeune, Paris 1927.

BARR (A. H.): *Vincent van Gogh*. Travelling exhibition. Museum of Modern Art, New York. 90 illustrations. Museum of Modern Art, New York 1935.

FLORISOONE (Michel). REWALD (John): *Van Gogh*. Exposition internationale (classe de Muséographie), Palais de Tokio, Paris 1937. Introduction and critical study by René Huyghe. 94 works reproduced. Special number of "Amour de l'Art", Denoël, Paris 1937.

COOPER (Douglas): *Van Gogh. An Illustrated Supplement to the Exhibition Catalogue*. Arts Council of Great Britain, London 1947. Preface by Philip James; critical studies by R. Fry and A. M. Hammacher. 84 illustrations of which 14 in colour.

GANS (L.): *Vincent van Gogh. 1853-1890*. Preface by A. M. Hammacher. Exhibition held at Munich, Haus der Kunst, in 1956. 166 works exhibited, all reproduced.

TRALBAUT (Dr. Mark Edo): *Vincent van Gogh. 1853-1890. Leben und Schaffen. Dokumentation, Gemälde, Zeichnungen*. Exhibition Villa Hügel, Essen 1957.

COLLECTIONS IN ENGLISH OF
VAN GOGH'S LETTERS

The Complete Letters of Vincent van Gogh
800 letters, 180 facsimile reproductions of letters containing drawings or sketches. 21 colour plates. 29 half-tone illustrations. 3 volumes. London 1958

Letters to Emile Bernard translated by Douglas Lord (pseudonym of Douglas Cooper) London and New York 1938

The Letters of Vincent van Gogh to his Brother, 1872-86 London and New York. Introduction and notes by Johanna van Gogh-Bonger

Further Letters of Vincent van Gogh to his Brother, 1886-90 London and New York. Introduction and notes by Johanna van Gogh-Bonger

Letter to an Artist; from Vincent van Gogh to Anton Ridder van Rappard New York 1936

Thannhauser, Henry: *Van Gogh and John Russell* 3 unpublished letters 1888-1890. "Burlington Magazine" 13 September 1938

PRINCIPAL WORKS ON VAN GOGH IN ENGLISH

BURRA, P. J. S. *Van Gogh* London 1934

COOPER, D. *Vincent van Gogh* (drawings and water colours) Basel and New York 1955

DU QUESNE-VAN GOGH, E. H. *Personal Recollections of Vincent van Gogh* London 1913

EARP, T. W. *Van Gogh* London and Edinburgh n.d.

ESTIENNE, C. *Van Gogh* New York 1953

GOLDSCHEIDER, L. J. UHDE, W. *Vincent van Gogh* London 1947

HAMMACHER, A. M. *Van Gogh, the land where he was born and raised* 54 illustrations The Hague 1953

HARTRICK, A. S. *Post-Impressionism, with some personal recollections of Vincent van Gogh and Gauguin* London 1916

JAMES, P. *Van Gogh 1853-1890* 12 illustrations London 1948

JEWELL, E. A. *Vincent van Gogh* New York 1946

MEIER-GRAEFE, J. *Vincent* 2 vols. 103 illustrations London 1922. 61 illustrations in American edition New York 1933

NORDENFALK, C. *Vincent van Gogh* London 1947
Van Gogh and Literature "Journal of the Warburg and Courtauld Institutes" 1947

PACH, W. *Vincent van Gogh. A Study of the Artist and his Work in Relation to his Time* 30 illustrations New York 1936

REWALD, J. *Post-Impressionism. From van Gogh to Gauguin* (chapters 1, 4, 7 and 8) New York 1956

SCHAPIRO, M. *Vincent van Gogh* 70 illustrations New York 1950

VAN GELDER, J. C. *The Potato Eaters* 18 illustrations London n.d.

Art News Annual, special van Gogh issue, 1950. Contributions by W. Gaunt, J. Rewald, S. Spender, J. Beer, M. Pease. Reprinted as album with 19 colour plates: *Van Gogh* New York 1953

INDEX

INDEX OF WORKS REPRODUCED

The Index is arranged in chronological order under the names of the places where the pictures were produced. Each entry is set out in the following manner: the title of the work; the number under which it appears in the La Faille catalogue (1928 edition); the method and size (the first figure being the height); the Collection or Gallery in which the work is at present; the page, or the number in the Catalogue of Works Reproduced. Colour plates are indicated by an asterisk.

LE BORINAGE AND BRUSSELS

August 1880–12 April 1881

Except for several drawings which date from August 1879, it is true to say that in the Spring of 1880 van Gogh first became conscious of his vocation as a painter. He was already 27 years old and there only remained ten more years for him to live. From this period only some fifteen drawings are known to us, the greater part of which were destroyed or lost. They represent studies of miners, landscapes and copies of works by Millet.

August 1880

The Sower (after Millet) F830
Pen and wash, heightened in green and
  white 18⅞″ × 14½″
  V. W. van Gogh Collection, Laren *p. 194*

1880-1881

The Road F836
Ink and pencil 7½″ × 8⅝″
  V. W. van Gogh Collection, Laren *p. 9*

Canal bank F834
Ink and pencil 8⅝″ × 6¾″
  V. W. van Gogh Collection, Laren *p. 11*

ETTEN

12 April 1881–30 December 1881

Some fifty drawings are recorded for this period in pencil, pen, charcoal, Indian ink and water-colours. They include eight studies for The Sower, scenes from everyday life and landscapes. Van Gogh's first attempts at painting—notably two still-lifes.

1881

Man sweeping F890
Water-colour and black chalk
  21⅝″ × 10¾″
  Kröller-Müller Rijksmuseum, Otterlo *p. 19*

Gate-Keeper's House F900
Charcoal with white highlights
  17¾″ × 23⅝″
  Kröller-Müller Rijksmuseum, Otterlo *Cat.*

June 1881

The Forge F1084
Ink-wash and pencil, heightened in
  white 14⅝″ × 10¼″
  Kröller-Müller Rijksmuseum, Otterlo *Cat. 1*

Marshland F845
Pen and pencil 9″ × 12¼″
  *J. P. Scholte-van Houten Collection,
  Lochem* *p. 14*

June-July 1881

Pastor Theodorus van Gogh F876
Pencil and Indian ink wash heightened
  with white 13″ × 9⅞″
  Private Collection, Delft *Cat. 2*

August 1881

Windmills near Dordrecht F850
Water-colour, pencil, black and green
  chalk heightened with white
  10¼″ × 23⅝″
  Kröller-Müller Rijksmuseum, Otterlo *Cat. 4*

September 1881

The Sower F865
Pencil heightened with colour
$24\frac{3}{8}'' \times 18''$
Kröller-Müller Rijksmuseum, Otterlo   Cat. 3

The Sower F852
Pen and wash $24'' \times 15\frac{3}{4}''$
Private Collection, Delft   p. 194

The Sowers F853
Pencil $12\frac{1}{4}'' \times 8\frac{1}{4}''$
V. W. van Gogh Collection, Laren   p. 195

Peasant sowing F862
Pencil and charcoal with white high-
lights $24'' \times 17\frac{3}{4}''$
Kröller-Müller Rijksmuseum, Otterlo   p. 195

October 1881

Young peasant with scythe F851
Black   chalk   and   water-colour
$18\frac{1}{2}'' \times 24''$
Kröller-Müller Rijksmuseum, Otterlo   p. 15

November 1881

Man by the fire F868
Charcoal with white and red highlights
$22'' \times 17\frac{3}{4}''$
Kröller-Müller Rijksmuseum, Otterlo   Cat. 6

December 1881

Still-life with Jug F1 bis
Oil on canvas $17\frac{7}{8}'' \times 22\frac{1}{2}''$ Cat. 7

THE HAGUE

31 December 1881–September 1883

Some twenty paintings, of fisherman and
peasants at work, sea and land-scapes. About
200 drawings and water-colours; of old
people in hospital; working-class women;
sowers; townscapes and views from his
studio at Schenkweg. He returns to the use
of chalk and Indian-ink. He produces fifteen
lithographs.

January 1882

Man digging F908
Pencil and ink $19\frac{5}{8}'' \times 11\frac{3}{8}''$
V. W. van Gogh Collection, Laren   p. 19

View of Scheveningen F1041
Pencil, water-colour and white chalk
$17\frac{3}{8}'' \times 23\frac{5}{8}''$
V. W. van Gogh Collection, Laren   Cat. 8

April 1882

The Widow F396
Pen, pencil and sepia $24'' \times 14\frac{5}{8}''$
Kröller-Müller Rijksmuseum, Otterlo   p. 29

Study of a Tree F933
Black chalk, pencil and water-colour
$19\frac{1}{4}'' \times 27\frac{1}{8}''$
Kröller-Müller Rijksmuseum, Otterlo   p. 21

May 1882

Behind the Schenkweg F939
Ink-wash and pencil heightened with
white $11\frac{3}{8}'' \times 18\frac{1}{2}''$
Kröller-Müller Rijksmuseum, Otterlo   Cat. 9

Fish drying (La Sècherie de Limandes)
F938
Pen, pencil and wash $11'' \times 17\frac{3}{8}''$
Kröller-Müller Rijksmuseum, Otterlo   p. 22

July 1882

Road near Loosduinen F1089
Pen and black chalk heightened with
white $10\frac{1}{4}'' \times 14\frac{1}{8}''$
V. W. van Gogh Collection, Laren   p. 23

* The Roofs. View from van Gogh's
studio in the Schenkweg F943
Water-colour heightened with white
$15\frac{3}{8}'' \times 21\frac{5}{8}''$
G. Renand Collection, Paris   p. 13

The Coast near Scheveningen
Oil on canvas stuck on cardboard
$13\frac{3}{4}'' \times 20\frac{1}{8}''$
Dr. E. Ribbius Peletier Collection,
Amsterdam   Cat. 10

September 1882

* Girl in Forest
Oil on canvas $15\frac{5}{8}'' \times 23\frac{1}{4}''$
Kröller-Müller Rijksmuseum, Otterlo   p. 17

October 1882

Old Man with an Umbrella F968
Pencil $19\frac{1}{4}'' \times 11''$
Mr. and Mrs. John Rewald Collection,
New York   p. 26

November 1882

Old Man weeping   F997
Pencil $19\frac{5}{8}'' \times 12\frac{1}{4}''$
V. W. van Gogh Collection, Laren   p. 220

Miners' Wives carrying Coal
Water-colour heightened with white
   $12\frac{5}{8}'' \times 19\frac{5}{8}''$
Kröller-Müller Rijksmuseum, Otterlo   Cat. 11

Sorrow   F1655
Lithograph $15\frac{5}{8}'' \times 11\frac{3}{8}''$
V. W. van Gogh Collection, Laren   p. 43

January-February 1883

Girl with a Shawl   F1007
Black chalk and pencil with white
   highlights $16\frac{7}{8}'' \times 9\frac{7}{8}''$
Kröller-Müller Rijksmuseum, Otterlo   Cat. 12

February 1883

The Old Sailor   F1010
Black chalk, pen and pencil heightened
   with white $18\frac{1}{8}'' \times 10\frac{1}{4}''$
Kröller-Müller Rijksmuseum, Otterlo   p. 29

March-April 1883

Woman Praying   F1053
Black chalk, pencil and wash height-
   ened with white $24\frac{3}{4}'' \times 15\frac{3}{4}''$
Kröller-Müller Rijksmuseum, Otterlo   Cat. 13

August 1883

Fisherman's Wife
Oil. Canvas on wood $20\frac{1}{8}'' \times 13''$
Kröller-Müller Rijksmuseum, Otterlo   Cat. 14

DRENTHE

September 1883–30 November 1883

A stay of three months in Drenthe resulted
in a dozen drawings and eight pictures.

September 1883

Peasant at Work   F12
Oil on wood $12\frac{1}{4}'' \times 11\frac{3}{4}''$
W. Weinberg Collection, Scarsdale, New
   York   Cat. 15

October 1883

Thatched Cottage
Oil on cardboard $15'' \times 21\frac{1}{4}''$
V. W. van Gogh Collection, Laren   Cat. 16

NUENEN

1 December 1883–27 November 1885

This period produced about 185 pictures,
a quarter of van Gogh's total work. About
forty characteristic landscapes (the garden of
a presbytery, a village church, the tower at
Nuenen, thatched cottages, avenues of trees
in Autumn) and as many still-lifes.

About 100 pictures of weavers and peasants
of which The Potato Eaters is the central work.

242 drawings are catalogued representing
roughly the same themes.

The Beginning of 1884

Van Gogh's family home at Nuenen
   (his studio on the right)
Pen and pencil heightened in white
   $9\frac{1}{2}'' \times 14\frac{1}{8}''$
Private Collection, Canada   p. 30

January 1884

The Weaver   F1108
Water-colour   Cat. 17

February 1884

The Weaver   F1123
Pen, heightened with white
   $12\frac{1}{4}'' \times 16\frac{1}{8}''$
V. W. van Gogh Collection, Laren   p. 46

March 1884

The Garden of the Presbytery at
   Nuènen. Winter   F1128
Pen and pencil $15\frac{5}{8}'' \times 20\frac{7}{8}''$
V. W. van Gogh Collection, Laren   p. 31

Avenue of Poplars   F1239
Indian ink and pencil $21\frac{1}{4}'' \times 15\frac{3}{8}''$
V. W. van Gogh Collection, Laren   p. 33

May 1884

Woman Spinning   F1139
Gouache $13'' \times 17\frac{3}{8}''$
Private Collection   Cat. 18

The Weaver F1107
Water-colour on paper 13⅜″ × 17⅝″
V. W. van Gogh Collection, Laren

The Loom F30
Oil on canvas 27⅝″ × 33½″
Kröller-Müller Rijksmuseum, Otterlo Cat. 19

The Weaver F1107
Water-colour on paper 13⅜″ × 17⅜″
V. W. van Gogh Collection, Laren Cat. 20

July 1884

Bullock Cart F38
Oil. Canvas on wood 22″ × 31⅞″
Kröller-Müller Rijksmuseum, Otterlo Cat. 21

August-September 1884

Snow Scene F43
Oil on wood 26⅜″ × 49⅝″
Private Collection, Haren Cat. 22

October 1884

Lane near Nuenen (completed at Paris in 1886) F45
Oil on canvas 30¾″ × 38⅝″
Boymans Museum, Rotterdam Cat. 23

November 1884

Still Life with Stone Bottles F50
Oil on canvas 13″ × 16½″
Kröller-Müller Rijksmuseum, Otterlo Cat. 25

Head of a Peasant smoking a Pipe F169
Oil on canvas 17⅜″ × 12⅝″
Kröller-Müller Rijksmuseum, Otterlo Cat. 26

Still Life with a Mortar F53
Oil. Canvas on wood 15¾″ × 22″
V. W. van Gogh Collection, Laren Cat. 27

Street in Eindhoven F1348
Water-colour 8¼″ × 11¾″
V. W. van Gogh Collection, Laren Cat. 24

Woman Digging F1258
Pen and charcoal 11⅜″ × 9″
V. W. van Gogh Collection, Laren p. 34

Woman planting F1280
Pencil 16⅞″ × 20½″
National Gallery, Oslo p. 35

The Farm F1345
Pencil 9½″ × 11¾″
V. W. van Gogh Collection, Laren p. 38

Studies (with the tower at Nuenen) F1336
Pencil and chalk 13¾″ × 8¼″
Kröller-Müller Rijksmuseum, Otterlo p. 39

March 1885

Peasant at Table F167
Oil on canvas 17⅜″ × 13″
Kröller-Müller Rijksmuseum, Otterlo Cat. 28

Peasant Woman Sweeping F152
Oil. Canvas on wood 16⅛″ × 10⅝″
Kröller-Müller Rijksmuseum, Otterlo Cat. 30

April 1885

Head of a Peasant Girl F138
Oil on canvas 13″ × 9″
P. Schmolka Collection, Prague Cat. 29

Peasant Woman in a Red Bonnet F160
Oil on canvas 16⅞″ × 11¾″
V. W. van Gogh Collection, Laren Cat. 31

Sunset F79
Oil on canvas 11″ × 16½″ Cat. 34

The Potato Eaters F78
Oil. Canvas on wood 28⅜″ × 36⅝″
Kröller-Müller Rijksmuseum, Otterlo Cat. 36

April-May 1885

Peasant Woman in a Brown Bonnet F154
Oil on canvas 15¾″ × 11¾″
Kröller-Müller Rijksmuseum, Otterlo Cat. 33

* The Potato Eaters F82
Oil on canvas 32¼″ × 44⅞″
V. W. van Gogh Collection, Laren p. 41

May 1885

Head of a Peasant Woman F86
Oil on canvas 16½″ × 13⅜″
Kröller-Müller Rijksmuseum, Otterlo Cat. 32

Cottage at Nightfall F83
Oil on canvas 25¼″ × 30¾″
V. W. van Gogh Collection, Laren Cat. 35

June 1885

Head of a Brabant Peasant Woman F388
Oil on canvas 16⅞″ × 14⅛″
V. W. van Gogh Collection, Laren Cat. 37

September 1885

Still Life with Potatoes F100
Oil on canvas $18\frac{1}{2}'' \times 23\frac{5}{8}''$
V. W. van Gogh Collection, Laren *Cat. 38*

Summer and Autumn 1885

Work in the Fields F129 bis
Oil on canvas $12\frac{1}{4}'' \times 15\frac{1}{2}''$
Kunsthaus, Zürich *Cat. 39*

Peasant Woman Washing Linen
F148
Oil on canvas $11\frac{5}{8}'' \times 14\frac{1}{8}''$
Formerly in the Gallery of Frans Buffa
and Son, Amsterdam *Cat. 40*

September-October 1885

Still-Life with Apples and Two
Gourds
Oil on canvas $23\frac{5}{8}'' \times 33\frac{1}{4}''$
Kröller-Müller Rijksmuseum, Otterlo *Cat. 41*

October 1885

Still-Life with Open Bible F117
Oil on canvas $25\frac{5}{8}'' \times 30\frac{3}{4}''$
V. W. van Gogh Collection, Laren *Cat. 42*

October-November 1885

The Presbytery at Nuenen F182
Oil on canvas $13'' \times 16\frac{7}{8}''$
V. W. van Gogh Collection, Laren *Cat. 43*

Lane in Autumn F122
Oil on canvas on wood $39'' \times 26''$
W. Nolst Trénité Collection, Rotterdam *Cat. 45*

Calendering F1337
Pen and lead pencil $9'' \times 11\frac{3}{4}''$
Kröller-Müller Rijksmuseum, Otterlo *p. 47*

November 1885

Autumn Landscape with Four Trees
F44
Oil on canvas $25\frac{1}{4}'' \times 35''$
Kröller-Müller Rijksmuseum, Otterlo *Cat. 44*

ANTWERP

28 November 1885-28 February 1886

From this period there are 12 paintings, of
which 2 are self-portraits, and about 40
drawings and sketches, mainly landscapes
and nudes.

Beginning of December 1885

Quay at Antwerp F211
Oil on panel
V. W. van Gogh Collection, Laren *p. 25*

December 1885

Self-portrait F180
Oil on canvas
V. W. van Gogh Collection, Laren *Cat. 46*

Working Girl F206
Oil on canvas
V. W. van Gogh Collection, Laren *Cat. 47*

PARIS

28 February 1886-20 February 1888

There are about 200 paintings from this
period, notably the following: 85 still-lifes,
of which 4 are studies of boots and 49
flower pieces. About 20 views of Montmartre, 31 studies of the outskirts of Paris
(Asnieres, la Grande Jatte, Chatou, Suresnes,
Bougival). Several portraits of men and
women. 23 self-portraits out of the 36 self-
portraits known to us. 3 Japonaiseries.
50 drawings, mainly nudes, views of Paris
and its environs.

1886

La Guinguette F238
Oil on canvas $19\frac{5}{8}'' \times 23\frac{1}{2}''$
Musée de l'Impressionisme, Paris *Cat. 48*

Reclining Nude F328
Oil on canvas $15'' \times 24''$
Mme. P. Goujon Collection, Paris *Cat. 49*

The Plaster Statuette F216
Oil on canvas $28\frac{3}{4}'' \times 21\frac{1}{4}''$
Mme. M. Feilchenfeldt Collection,
Zürich *Cat. 51*

The Moulin de la Galette F274
Oil on canvas $18\frac{1}{8}'' \times 15''$
Art Gallery and Museum, Glasgow *Cat. 52*

The Moulin de la Galette F227
Oil on canvas $14\frac{5}{8}'' \times 17\frac{3}{4}''$
Kröller-Müller Rijksmuseum, Otterlo *Cat. 53*

Montmartre F230
Oil on canvas 22" × $24\frac{3}{8}$"
V. W. van Gogh Collection, Laren Cat. 54

* Boots with Laces F255
Oil on canvas 15" × $18\frac{1}{8}$"
V. W. van Gogh Collection, Laren p. 36

The Terrace of the Tuileries F223
Oil on canvas $10\frac{5}{8}$" × $18\frac{1}{8}$"
Leicester Gallery, London Cat. 60

The Terrace of the Tuileries F1383
Lead pencil $3\frac{7}{8}$" × $6\frac{1}{4}$"
V. W. van Gogh Collection, Laren p. 67

The Garden of the Tuileries F1384
Lead pencil $4\frac{3}{8}$" × $7\frac{7}{8}$"
V. W. van Gogh Collection, Laren p. 69

The Bois de Boulogne F224
Oil on canvas $18\frac{1}{2}$" × $14\frac{5}{8}$"
Dr. Emil Hahnloser Collection, Zürich Cat. 61

Montmartre. The Street Lamps F272
Oil on canvas $17\frac{3}{8}$" × $13\frac{3}{8}$"
Art Institute, Chicago Cat. 50

* The Moulin de la Galette F348
Oil on canvas 24" × $19\frac{5}{8}$"
Museo Nacional de Bellas Artes, Buenos-Aires p. 45

Summer 1886

Red Gladioli F237
Oil on canvas 26" × $13\frac{3}{4}$"
Van Beuningen Collection, Vierhouten Cat. 55

Fritillaries in a Copper Vase F213
Oil on canvas $29\frac{1}{8}$" × 24"
Musée de l'Impressionisme, Paris Cat. 56

Hollyhocks F235
Oil on canvas 37" × $20\frac{1}{8}$"
Kunsthaus, Zürich Cat. 57

Roses and Sunflowers F250
Oil on canvas $19\frac{5}{8}$" × 24"
Kunsthalle, Mannheim Cat. 58

1886-1887

Shoes F331
Oil on cardboard 13" × $16\frac{1}{8}$"
V. W. van Gogh Collection, Laren Cat. 59

Portrait of Alexander Reid F343
Oil on cardboard $16\frac{1}{8}$" × 13"
J. A. McNeill Reid Collection, London Cat. 62

Self-portrait. Sketch F1378
Pen $12\frac{5}{8}$" × $9\frac{7}{8}$"
V. W. van Gogh Collection, Laren p. 59

Self-portrait F179
Oil on canvas $16\frac{1}{2}$" × $12\frac{1}{4}$"
V. W. van Gogh Collection, Laren Cat. 70

* Montmartre Fête F347
Oil on canvas $13\frac{3}{4}$" × $25\frac{1}{4}$"
V. W. van Gogh Collection, Laren p. 57

1887

* Boots F333
Oil on canvas 13" × $16\frac{1}{8}$"
Cone Collection, Museum of Art, Baltimore p. 37

* View of an Industrial Town F1410
Watercolour on paper $15\frac{3}{8}$" × $21\frac{1}{4}$"
Stedelijk Museum, Amsterdam p. 49

Absinth F339
Oil on canvas $18\frac{1}{2}$" × 13"
V. W. van Gogh Collection, Laren Cat. 63

Boulevard de Clichy F292
Oil on canvas $18\frac{1}{4}$" × $15\frac{1}{8}$"
V. W. van Gogh Collection, Laren Cat. 65

View from Van Gogh's Room, Rue Lepic F341
Oil on canvas $18\frac{1}{8}$" × 15"
V. W. van Gogh Collection, Laren Cat. 66

* Montmartre Gardens in Winter F346
Oil on canvas $16\frac{7}{8}$" × $31\frac{1}{2}$"
V. W. van Gogh Collection, Laren p. 73

Self-portrait F268
Oil on canvas $16\frac{1}{8}$" × $13\frac{1}{4}$"
John Quinn Collection, New York Cat. 69

Self-portrait F178
Oil on canvas $20\frac{1}{2}$" × $16\frac{3}{4}$"
Municipal Museum, The Hague Cat. 71

Self-portrait F356
Oil on canvas $16\frac{1}{8}$" × 13"
V. W. van Gogh Collection, Laren Cat. 72

Self-portrait F344
Oil on canvas $17\frac{3}{8}$" × $14\frac{3}{4}$"
V. W. van Gogh Collection, Laren Cat. 73

Self-portrait F380
Oil on paper $12\frac{5}{8}$" × 9"
Kröller-Müller Rijksmuseum, Otterlo Cat. 74

1887-1888

The Woman at Le Tambourin   F370
Oil on canvas $21\frac{7}{8}'' \times 18\frac{1}{4}''$
V. W. van Gogh Collection, Laren   *Cat. 93*

January-February 1888

Japonaiserie: The Actor (after Keisai
  Yeisen)   F373
Oil on canvas $41\frac{3}{8}'' \times 24''$
V. W. van Gogh Collection, Laren   *Cat. 94*

Japonaiserie: The Bridge (after
  Hiroshige)   F372
Oil on canvas $28\frac{3}{4}'' \times 21\frac{1}{8}''$
V. W. van Gogh Collection, Laren   *Cat. 96*

Self-Portrait at the Easel   F522
Oil on canvas $28\frac{5}{8}'' \times 19\frac{7}{8}''$
V. W. van Gogh Collection, Laren   *Cat. 97*

ARLES

21 February 1888–3 May 1889

There are 190 paintings from this period:
17 orchards in blossom. 80 landscapes
comprising the series of the *Pont de l'Anglois*,
seascapes, boats and farmhouses at Les
Saintes-Maries, different views of Arles,
harvests, stacks in the plain of La Crau,
gardens in the town or at the hospital,
vineyards. 17 flower pieces, including the
series of *Sunflowers*. 40 portraits, including
those of the Roulin family, Lieutenant
Milliet, the painter Boch, the Arlésienne,
and Dr. Rey. 11 still-lifes. 7 interiors, including the *All Night Café*, *Van Gogh's Chair*,
Gauguin's Armchair, *Van Gogh's Room*.
4 sowers. 7 self-portraits. 108 catalogued
drawings, many of which are preparatory
studies for paintings.

February 1888

* The Arles country under snow
  F290
Oil on canvas $15\frac{3}{4}'' \times 18\frac{7}{8}''$
*Mr. and Mrs. Justin K. Thannhauser
  Collection, New York*   *p. 77*

Snow at Arles   F391
Oil on canvas $19\frac{5}{8}'' \times 23\frac{5}{8}''$ *Cat. 98*

Sprig of Almond Blossom   F392
Oil on canvas $9\frac{1}{2}'' \times 7\frac{1}{2}''$
V. W. van Gogh Collection, Laren   *Cat. 99*

March 1888

The Footpath   F1499
Pencil and pen $10\frac{1}{4}'' \times 13\frac{3}{4}''$
V. W. van Gogh Collection, Laren   *p. 79*

View of the Viaduct at Arles   F398
Oil on canvas $17\frac{3}{4}'' \times 19\frac{1}{4}''$
Musée Rodin, Paris   *Cat. 100*

The Pont de Gleize, Vigueyret Canal,
  near Arles   F396
Oil on canvas $18\frac{1}{8}'' \times 19\frac{1}{4}''$
Private Collection   *Cat. 101*

Letter to Emile Bernard, with a
  sketch: Le Pont de l'Anglois   *p. 83*

Le Pont de l'Anglois   F1470
Pen $12\frac{1}{4}'' \times 18\frac{1}{2}''$ *p. 86*

* Le Pont de l'Anglois   F400
Oil on canvas $23\frac{1}{4}'' \times 28\frac{3}{4}''$
V. W. van Gogh Collection, Laren   *p. 80*

Le Pont de l'Anglois   F1471
Pen $9\frac{1}{2}'' \times 12\frac{5}{8}''$
*Mr. and Mrs. George Gard de Sylva
  Collection, County Museum, Los Angeles*
  p. 87

Le Pont de l'Anglois   F397
Oil on canvas $20\frac{1}{2}'' \times 24\frac{3}{4}''$
Kröller-Müller Rijksmuseum, Otterlo   *Cat. 102*

March-April 1888

* Le Pont de l'Anglois   F1480
Watercolour $11\frac{3}{4}'' \times 11\frac{3}{4}''$
Private Collection, Berlin   *p. 84*

Roofs
Pencil and pen $9\frac{7}{8}'' \times 13\frac{3}{8}''$
*Mr. and Mrs. John Rewald Collection,
  New York*   *p. 89*

About April 1888

The Tile Works   F1500
Ink and chalk $10\frac{1}{4}'' \times 13\frac{3}{4}''$
Courtauld Institute, London   *p. 95*

April 1888

* Le Pont de l'Anglois   F571
Oil on canvas $23\frac{1}{4}'' \times 24\frac{3}{4}''$
Wildenstein Gallery, New York   *p. 85*

SAINT-REMY

3 May 1889–16 May 1890

In spite of the three nervous breakdowns van Gogh had been through and the great difficulty he found in working, there are more than 150 paintings for this year alone, including: Some hundred landscapes and exteriors. The grounds of the Asylum. A cornfield seen from his bedroom. Cypresses. Alpine landscapes. Paintings showing harvest scenes and olive groves. Several flower pieces. 6 portraits, among them being the *Chief Superintendent*. 4 self-portraits. 38 canvases inspired by the work of Millet, Delacroix, Gustave Doré, Daumier, Rembrandt, Gauguin. Some 100 drawings and water-colours.

Irises F608
Oil on canvas 28″ × 36⅝″
Mrs. Charles S. Peyson Collection, New York — *Cat. 170*

Garden in Provence F1501
Ink and pencil on rose-coloured paper 18⅞″ × 24⅜″
V. W. van Gogh Collection, Laren — *p. 187*

The Stone Bench in the Hospital Gardens F1522
Pen and pencil 24¾″ × 18½″
V. W. van Gogh Collection, Laren — *p. 199*

The Fountain in the Garden of the Hospital at Saint-Rémy F1531
Pen 18⅞″ × 17¾″
V. W. van Gogh Collection, Laren — *p. 203*

May-June 1889

* Young Male Peasant F531
Oil on canvas 24″ × 19⅝″
E. Sforni Collection, Florence — *p. 173*

The Garden of the Asylum at Saint-Rémy F734
Oil on canvas 37⅜″ × 29¾″
Kröller-Müller Rijksmuseum, Otterlo — *Cat. 174*

June 1889

Corridor in the Asylum of Saint-Rémy F1529
Gouache and water-colour 25⅝″ × 19¼″
Museum of Modern Art, New York — *Cat. 175*

The Cornfield F1548
Pen 18⅛″ × 24″
G. Serigiers Collection, Brussels — *p. 207*

Ripening Corn F719
Oil on canvas 28¾″ × 36¼″
State Museum, Prague — *Cat. 172*

Cornfield and Cypresses F615
Oil on canvas 28⅜″ × 35⅞″
Courtauld Bequest, Tate Gallery, London — *Cat. 173*

Cornfield with Reaper F618
Oil on canvas 29⅛″ × 36¼″
V. W. van Gogh Collection, Laren — *Cat. 171*

Cornfield in the Alpilles F1547
Pen 18½″ × 24⅜″
V. W. van Gogh Collection, Laren — *p. 215*

Cypresses by Moonlight F1540
Pen 18½″ × 24¾″
Kunsthalle, Bremen — *p. 176*

* Starry Night F612
Oil on canvas 28¾″ × 36¼″
Museum of Modern Art, New York — *p. 177*

Cypresses F1525
Pen 24¾″ × 18½″
Brooklyn Museum, New York — *p. 210*

Two Women and Cypresses (finished in February 1890) F620
Oil on canvas 35⅞″ × 28″
Kröller-Müller Rijksmuseum, Otterlo — *Cat. 176*

June-July 1889

* Hills at Saint-Rémy F622
Oil on canvas 28¾″ × 36⅝″
Mr. and Mrs. Justin K. Thannhauser Collection, New York — *p. 168*

Olive Trees F712
Oil on canvas 28½″ × 36¼″
John Hay Whitney Collection, New York — *Cat. 177*

September 1889

Pietà (after Delacroix) F630
Oil on canvas 28¾″ × 23⅞″
V. W. van Gogh Collection, Laren — *Cat. 181*

* Vincent's Room F482
Oil on canvas 24⅜″ × 35⅜″
V. W. van Gogh Collection, Laren — *p. 181*

January 1890

* Schoolboy   F665
Oil on canvas $24\frac{3}{4}'' \times 21\frac{1}{4}''$
Museum of Art, Sao Paolo   *p. 205*

January-February 1890

L'Arlésienne (after a drawing by
  Gauguin)   F540
Oil on canvas $23\frac{5}{8}'' \times 19\frac{5}{8}''$
*H. P. Bremmer Collection, Stedelijk
  Museum, Amsterdam*   *Cat. 193*

February 1890

* Prisoners at Exercise (after Gustave
  Doré)   F669
Oil on canvas $31\frac{1}{2}'' \times 25\frac{1}{4}''$
Pushkin Museum, Moscow   *p. 209*

April 1890

Hovels (Memories of the North)
  F673
Oil on canvas $17\frac{7}{8}'' \times 16\frac{7}{8}''$
Private Collection, The Hague   *Cat. 192*

* Peasants at Work (after Millet)
  F694
Oil on canvas $12\frac{5}{8}'' \times 16\frac{1}{8}''$
*Mr. and Mrs. Justin K. Thannhauser
  Collection, New York*   *p. 197*

* The Fenced Field   F720
Oil on canvas $28'' \times 35\frac{7}{8}''$
Kröller-Müller Rijksmuseum, Otterlo   *p. 213*

Spring 1890

Hyacinth Stalks   F1612
Pen and pencil $16\frac{1}{8}'' \times 12\frac{1}{4}''$
V. W. van Gogh Collection, Laren   *p. 235*

Arum Lilies   F1613
Pen $12\frac{1}{4}'' \times 16\frac{1}{8}''$
V. W. van Gogh Collection, Laren   *p. 242*

April-May 1890

At the Foot of the Alpilles   F724
Oil on canvas $22\frac{1}{4}'' \times 28''$
Kröller-Müller Rijksmuseum, Otterlo   *Cat. 194*

Field of Red Poppies   F581
Oil on canvas $28'' \times 35\frac{7}{8}''$
Kunsthalle, Bremen   *Cat. 195*

May 1890

* Tree-Trunks   F676
Oil on canvas $28\frac{3}{8}'' \times 35\frac{3}{8}''$
Kröller-Müller Rijksmuseum, Otterlo   *p. 201*

Resurrection of Lazarus (after
  Rembrandt)   F677
Oil on canvas $19\frac{1}{8}'' \times 24\frac{3}{4}''$
V. W. van Gogh Collection, Laren   *Cat. 196*

* The Threshold of Eternity   F702
Oil on canvas $31\frac{1}{2}'' \times 25\frac{1}{4}''$
Kröller-Müller Rijksmuseum, Otterlo   *p. 221*

Road with Cypresses   F683
Oil on canvas $35\frac{7}{8}'' \times 28''$
Kröller-Müller Rijksmuseum, Otterlo   *Cat. 197*

White Roses   F681
Oil on canvas $28'' \times 35\frac{3}{8}''$
*Mr. and Mrs. W. Averill Harriman
  Collection, New York*   *Cat. 198*

* Irises   F678
Oil on canvas $36\frac{1}{4}'' \times 29\frac{1}{4}''$
V. W. van Gogh Collection, Laren   *p. 225*

AUVERS-SUR-OISE

20 May 1890–29 July 1890

During the last two months of his life,
Vincent achieved no less than 32 drawings
and 70 canvases, of which 15 were portraits
or studies of various people, 3 were still-lifes
and the rest were mainly landscapes or views
of Auvers (farms, thatched cottages, village
houses). He made one etching, the *Portrait
of Dr. Gachet.*

May 1890

Chestnut Tree in Blossom   F752
Oil on canvas $24'' \times 18\frac{7}{8}''$
Kröller-Müller Rijksmuseum, Otterlo   *Cat. 199*

Dr. Gachet's Garden (27 May)   F755
Oil on canvas $28\frac{3}{8}'' \times 20\frac{1}{2}''$
Musée de l'Impressionisme, Paris   *Cat. 201*

INDEX OF NAMES